FREE LA

The Ultimate
FREE FUN GUIDE™
to the City of Angels

CorleyGuide™

Free L.A.

Contributors

ROBERT STOCK
ALISHA L. SEMCHUCK
JOE TORTOMASI
SUSAN CARRIER
DESIREE ZAMORANO
RON O'BRIEN

Editor

TROY CORLEY

BOOK DESIGN BY KATHY KIKKERT

Attention corporations, organizations and
foundations. *FREE L.A.* is perfect for fundraisers,
premiums and gifts.

Contact the publisher:

CorleyGuide™

P.O. Box 381
Ojai, CA 93024
805-646-5467
FAX: 1-877-376-2668
www.freela.net
booksales@freela.net

Publisher's Cataloging-in-Publication Data

Free L.A. : the ultimate free fun guide to the city of
angels / Troy Corley, editor; [contributors, Robert
Stock ... et al.]
p. cm.
Includes index.

ISBN 0-97062-421-2

1. Family recreation—California—Los Angeles—
Guidebooks. 2. Family recreation—California,
Southern—Guidebooks. 3. Los Angeles (Calif.)—
Guidebooks. 4. California, Southern—Guidebooks. I.
Corley, Troy. II. Stock, Robert, 1953 - III. Free LA :
the ultimate free fun guide to the city of angels.

F869.L83 C67917.9494—dc22   2004107135

Printed in the United States of America

Acknowledgements

*

THANKS TO THE *FREE L.A.* CREW OF WRITERS WHO helped research and write up the FREE events and venues in this guide. Special thanks to prolific contributor Robert Stock, who was always there for *FREE L.A.*

A big bouquet of gratitude to book designer Kathy Kikkert who gave *FREE L.A.* its colorful and unique style.

To Shannon Bell, marketing consultant and Jerry Eriks, office manager, thanks for pitching in when and where needed.

Thanks to all those foundations, organizations, individuals, government agencies and corporations who provide funding and person power to make FREE fun available in LA. A special acknowledgement is in order for the LA Convention and Visitors Bureau, the city Cultural Affairs Department and the city Department of Recreation & Parks. In particular at the latter, public relations officer Harvey Drut, who never failed to answer my questions.

Last, but never least, a great deal of thanks and hugs to my partner in life and in business, Ron O'Brien, and to my two children, Tristan and Emelia, who put up with a lot during the course of producing this first edition of *FREE L.A.*

—Troy Corley

CONTENTS

HOW TO USE THIS BOOK

WHO DOESN'T LIKE TO DO FUN THINGS FOR FREE?
Los Angeles and the communities surrounding the City of
Angels are full of **FREE events and venues** from Hollywood
to Malibu to Pasadena. *FREE L.A.* gives you the scoop on
hundreds of them from FREE festivals and films to FREE
museums and gardens.

FREE L.A. makes it easy to find the FREE fun. The guide
is divided into **five** sections: **Annual Events, Holiday
Events, Extra Events, Venues** and **Indexes**.

ANNUAL EVENTS has ethnic fiestas, nature festivals,
flower, gem and car shows, aviation expos, community
parades, sand sculpture contests and fishing derbies. It
gives you the details on the FREE fun in 12 chapters—
from January to December.

HOLIDAY EVENTS includes Lunar New Year parades,
Earth Day festivals, Cinco de Mayo fiestas, July 4th fireworks, Halloween howls and Christmas boat parades.

EXTRA EVENTS features more FREE fun—concerts,
films, gardening goodies and ongoing happenings.

VENUES has detailed information on dozens of FREE
museums, museums with FREE admission days and botanical gardens.

Each event and venue also comes with the unique
Thomas Guide® Page & Grid™ map coordinates. Rand
McNally's® Thomas Guide provides a quick and easy way to

navigate LA's freeway maze. You'll find the **Page & Grid** information right underneath each event and venue.

FREE L.A. offers other **visitor tips** such as information on **parking.** If there's anything in short supply in LA, it's FREE parking. Yet many events and venues do provide FREE parking. We let you know. You'll also find out if you have to pay big bucks for a parking space, or if a FREE shuttle is available.

Want to know if an event is **kid-friendly**, **historic** or offers **wheelchair** or **stroller access**? We've noted that information, too. And it's all spelled out. No funky icons to scratch your head over.

INDEXES provides two more ways to find an event, venue or place in *FREE L.A.* The **Main Index** lets you search for all of *FREE L.A.*'s events and venues alphabetically. Look in the **Location Index** to find FREE fun by community, be it Long Beach, Santa Clarita or Woodland Hills. The **Thomas Guide Page** for that area is also included.

About Free

Most of the places and events listed in *FREE L.A.* are **FREE** to the public because they are funded through government grants, corporate sponsorships, non-profit groups' fundraising efforts and individual donations. In fact, you might be asked for a donation at any one of the venues. Consider it. A dollar in their donation bucket wouldn't hurt.

If you really like going to a particular museum or cultural institution, think about paying for an **annual membership**. Most museums offer them and memberships are sized for individuals, seniors and families. Show your membership card at the door and you get in FREE no matter how many times you show up. With some museums hosting several new exhibits a year or special holiday events, you'll be able to see and do it all without paying an admission charge each time. For some museums, a one-time visit for a group of four equals the cost of a single annual membership.

Memberships also come with **other perks**: discounts on gift shop merchandise; discounts on lectures, workshops and seminars; first in line for special exhibition tickets and special members-only events.

A reminder about **scheduling**. Everything is **subject to change**. Before you get your heart set on a FREE Chinese New Year's celebration or on a FREE garden tour, call ahead. Check the **Web site** listed for the event or venue. Confirm the **hours** and the **parking** information. What's here today could be gone tomorrow. But for those of us who love seeing LA for FREE, let's hope not!

Thanks and enjoy our Free Fun Guide, *FREE L.A.!*

Annual Events

Día de Los Tres Reyes (The Day of Three Kings)

EL PUEBLO DE LOS ANGELES HISTORIC MONUMENT
125 Paseo de la Plaza (Olvera Street), LA 90012
213-625-5045
www.olvera-street.com

Celebrate the Epiphany—the arrival of the Three Kings to the nativity—at this traditional Mexican holiday held the twelfth day after Christmas. In Mexican families, many children receive their Christmas gifts on this day, so Olvera Street merchants join the gift-giving spirit by handing out prizes; FREE *champurado,* a Mexican chocolate drink; and *pan dulce,* Mexican sweet bread. Kids break a treat-filled *piñata* and scramble for the candy when it opens. Evening festivities include music and a colorful marketplace procession.

WHEN: Jan 6
PARKING: Metered street, pay lots ∗ **THOMAS GUIDE:** 634 G3
KID-FRIENDLY ∗ **HISTORIC** ∗ **WHEELCHAIR/STROLLER ACCESS**

Kingdom Day Parade

MARTIN LUTHER KING, JR. BLVD
@ Crenshaw Blvd, LA 90008
213-487-2882
www.kingdayinla.homestead.com

Cheer for the ideals of peace and prosperity at one of the largest celebrations of the national holiday that commemorates the life of slain Civil Rights leader Dr. Martin Luther King, Jr. Join more than 100,000 believers in "The Dream" as they line the two-mile parade route that starts at Crenshaw and King Boulevards. The three-hour parade includes peace marchers, labor leaders, civil rights activists, marching bands, drill teams, equestrian units and martial arts teams. The parade is televised on NBC4. Look for Rep. Maxine Waters (D-Los Angeles) who walks the entire 20-block route.

WHEN: King Day, 3rd Mon in Jan
PARKING: Metered street, pay lots * **THOMAS GUIDE:** 673 E2
KID-FRIENDLY * **HISTORIC** * **WHEELCHAIR/STROLLER ACCESS**

Little Tokyo New Year

WELLER COURT
Second and San Pedro Streets, LA 90012
213-626-3067
www.jccsc.com

Witness the ancient ceremony of *kagamiwari* or sake barrel breaking, a tradition that is thought to bring health, wealth and happiness to those who attend. The ceremony is part of the New Year's festivities at Weller Court, a shopping area located near the New Otani Hotel. Sponsored by the Japanese Chamber of Commerce of Southern California, the celebration includes *taiko* drum performances, *kendo* demonstrations, a Lion Dance and *kimono* show.

Participate in *hanetsuki,* a Japanese New Year's game and watch *mochitsuki,* the traditional pounding of sweet rice. Gifts are given to the first 300 children who arrive.

WHEN: Jan 1
PARKING: Metered street, pay lots ＊ **THOMAS GUIDE:** 634 G4
KID-FRIENDLY ＊ **WHEELCHAIR/STROLLER ACCESS**

Long Beach Martin Luther King, Jr. Parade

MARTIN LUTHER KING, JR. PARK
1950 Lemon Ave, Long Beach 90806
562-570-4405
www.ci.long-beach.ca.us

Discover unity and the power of peace as thousands gather to watch a parade honoring Nobel Peace Prize winner Dr. Martin Luther King, Jr. Organized by the Sixth Council District, the parade commemorates King's devotion to civil rights. Floats, marching bands and local civic and political leaders join the parade route that starts at Anaheim St. and Martin Luther King Ave. The procession ends at Martin Luther King, Jr. Park where the celebration continues through the afternoon with a multi-cultural food fair and FREE activities and games for kids. Best parking bet: Long Beach City College parking lot at PCH and Orange Ave with FREE parade shuttle.

WHEN: Sat before King Day (3rd Mon in Jan)
PARKING: FREE ＊ **THOMAS GUIDE:** 795 F4
KID-FRIENDLY ＊ **HISTORIC** ＊ **WHEELCHAIR/STROLLER ACCESS**

Oshogatsu: New Year Family Day Festival

JAPANESE AMERICAN NATIONAL MUSEUM

369 E 1st St, Little Tokyo, LA 90012

213-625-0414

www.janm.org

Greet the New Year by learning about Japanese traditions and symbols at this family-oriented celebration. A highlight of the afternoon event is watching *mochitsuki,* a traditional rice pounding performance accompanied by the rhythmic sounds of *taiko* drums. The rice is used to make *mochi*—sweet rice cakes—a special Japanese treat. Participate in arts & craft classes, listen to *Oshogatsu* storytelling and watch an Iaido demonstration—the art of Japanese swordsmanship.

WHEN: Jan 1
PARKING: Metered street, $4 to $6 pay lots * **THOMAS GUIDE:** 634 G4
KID-FRIENDLY * **WHEELCHAIR/STROLLER ACCESS**

Shikishi Exhibit

JAPANESE AMERICAN CULTURAL AND COMMUNITY CENTER

George J. Doizaki Gallery

244 S San Pedro St, Little Tokyo, LA 90012

213-628-2725

www.jaccc.org

Welcome the New Year at this annual community display of 250+ traditional Japanese New Year greeting cards known as *shikishi* or wall hangings. Each year the collection includes *shikishi* created by local artists, community leaders, Japanese celebrities and dignitaries. The public is invited to contribute to the display by creating artwork on a standard blank *shikishi,* made of special paper attached to a board. The exhibit lasts through January.

WHEN: Jan 1–Jan 30
PARKING: Lots across the street * **THOMAS GUIDE:** 634 G4
KID-FRIENDLY * **WHEELCHAIR/STROLLER ACCESS**

Tournament of Roses Family Festival

ROSE BOWL STADIUM
1001 Rose Bowl Dr, Pasadena 91103
626-449-ROSE
www.tournamentofroses.com

Fill the void between Christmas and New Year's Day
(December 28 through 31) by marching the family to
Pasadena's annual celebration of football, floats and
family. Witness the final stages of Rose Parade float decorating, play organized games, tour the Tournament of
Roses Museum, munch on FREE food samples, and participate in FREE, hands-on craft projects, from making paper
roses to building a bird house. Most events are FREE,
but others, such as Equefest and the museum, charge
admission.

WHEN: Dec 28 – Dec 31
PARKING: FREE at Rose Bowl * **THOMAS GUIDE:** 565 F2
KID-FRIENDLY

Tournament of Roses Parade

COLORADO BLVD
between Orange Grove and Sierra Madre Blvd, Pasadena
626-449-ROSE
www.tournamentofroses.com

Eager to view Pasadena's annual spectacle from a closer
vantage point than the living room sofa? No need to purchase grandstand seating or camp out overnight to enjoy
the New Year's tradition with 100+ floats, bands and
equestrian units. Here's how: Driver drops off kids, an

adult, chairs and hot cocoa at a designated spot along Colorado Blvd. The eastern part of the route tends to be less crowded. Driver parks in a residential area north of Colorado Blvd. Driver walks (or scooters) approximately one mile to the designated spot and joins the family (and nearly one million other parade route spectators) for the "mother of all parades." Then ooh and ahh over the floats exquisitely and exclusively decorated with roses and other beautiful botanicals.

WHEN: Jan 1
PARKING: FREE, north of Colorado Blvd * **THOMAS GUIDE:** 566 C4
KID-FRIENDLY * **WHEELCHAIR/STROLLER ACCESS**

Whale Fiesta

CABRILLO MARINE AQUARIUM
3720 Stephen White Dr, San Pedro 90731
310-548-7562
www.cabrilloaq.org

Celebrate the return of Pacific Gray Whales to Southern California's coast. A tradition since 1971, this festival features the aquarium's Whalewatch Naturalists, marine mammal experts and often a special appearance by John Olguin, CMA Director Emeritus. Attend informal talks, slide shows and lectures on the whales' massive migration southward. Kids crawl through a life-sized inflated whale and create cetacean crafts. Enter the Great Duct Tape Whale Contest or spout out at the Whale Poets corner. More than 15 marine mammal awareness groups offer FREE materials and information.

WHEN: Sun in Jan, date varies
PARKING: FREE at 22nd and Minor Streets with FREE shuttle; $5 at Cabrillo Beach
THOMAS GUIDE: 854 C2
KID-FRIENDLY
WHEELCHAIR/STROLLER ACCESS

Note
FIND FREE LUNAR NEW YEAR EVENTS UNDER HOLIDAYS
*

FEBRUARY

Camellia Festival

TEMPLE CITY PARK
9701 Las Tunas Dr, Temple City 91780
626-297-9150
www.templecitychamber.org

Bursting into full bloom this month, red, pink and variegated blossoms blanket Temple City also known as "Home of Camellias." Given that name in 1944 by the local Women's Club, the flowerful festival and parade promote family life in the San Gabriel Valley community. About 5,000 kids from area youth groups design and build non-motorized floats using Camellias to accent their creations. Held the last Saturday in February, the parade draws 20,000 spectators who cheer on the kids as they push their floats down Las Tunas Drive. A three-day carnival takes place at Temple City Park.

WHEN: Last Sat in Feb
PARKING: FREE ★ **THOMAS GUIDE:** 597 A3
KID-FRIENDLY ★ **WHEELCHAIR/STROLLER ACCESS**

Black History Parade & Festival

JACKIE ROBINSON CENTER

1020 N Fair Oaks Ave, Pasadena 91103

626-744-7300

www.ci.pasadena.ca.us

Celebrate African American achievements and share in the pride. The parade route begins at the center and ends at the park honoring one of Pasadena's legends: Jackie Robinson. A 20- year tradition, Grand Marshals have included Mr. T and Dorian Gregory. Discover great inventors at the FREE mobile Black Inventions Museum. Learn about Benjamin Bradley who invented a working steam engine in the 1840s for a war sloop, or Otis Boykin who created resistors for computers, radios, and television. Afterwards, look around the booths, shop, grab a bite.

WHEN: 3rd Sat of Feb
PARKING: FREE * **THOMAS GUIDE:** 565 H2
KID-FRIENDLY

Lantern Festival

CHINESE AMERICAN MUSEUM

425 N Los Angeles St, LA 90012

213-626-5240

www.camla.org

Light the way to the New Year during this traditional Chinese festival, held around the fifteenth day of the first lunar month. The festival includes FREE live dance, musical and acrobatic performances. Sponsored by the newly opened Chinese American Museum, the festivities take place at the nearby El Pueblo de Los Angeles Historical Monument, across from Union Station. Learn about *feng shui*, Chinese calligraphy and lantern making at the tradi-

tional arts & crafts booths. Grade school children participate in a lantern contest, march in a lantern parade and
listen to stories told in Chinese, Spanish and English.

WHEN: Around 15th day of 1st lunar month
PARKING: $5 lots * **THOMAS GUIDE:** 634 G3
KID-FRIENDLY * **HISTORIC** * **WHEELCHAIR/STROLLER ACCESS**

LA Times Travel Show

LONG BEACH CONVENTION CENTER
300 E Ocean Blvd, Long Beach 90802
562-436-3661 (Convention Center)
www.latimes.com

Are you a travel agent? If so you can get into the travel
event of the year for FREE. Just show your ASTA or IATA
card, register at the door and you can spend two days visiting with hundreds of travel exhibitors. Come between 8AM
to 10AM the first day and beat the rush. Bring a friend for
FREE too! FREE gifts for travel agents on Saturday, while
supplies last. If you're not a travel agent, or don't know
one, bring an LA Times Travel Show ad for a discounted
admission.

WHEN: Feb weekend, date varies
PARKING: $8 * **THOMAS GUIDE:** 825 E1

Pan African Film and Arts Festival ArtFest

BALDWIN HILLS CRENSHAW PLAZA
3650 W Martin Luther King, Jr. Blvd, LA 90008
323-295-1706 (PAFF Office)
www.paff.org

Cultivate your artistic side at one of the nation's largest
exhibits of fine arts featuring prominent and emerging

Black artists and craftspeople. Held in conjunction with the Pan African Film and Arts Festival, the highlighted works of 60+ artisans are on display for two weeks, occupying two plaza floors. View sculptures, mixed media, paintings and drawings. Look over unique pieces of wearable art from one-of-a-kind jewelry pieces to designer apparel.

WHEN: 1st two weeks in Feb
PARKING: FREE * **THOMAS GUIDE:** 673 E2
KID-FRIENDLY * **WHEELCHAIR/STROLLER ACCESS**

Pan African Film and Arts Festival Children's Festivals

MAGIC JOHNSON THEATRES
4020 Marlton Ave, LA 90008
323-295-1706 (PAFF Office)
www.paff.org

Screen award-winning movies and animated features during these Saturday morning shows set aside for children and their parents during the two-week run of the Pan African Film and Arts Festival. Storytelling, hands-on activities and refreshments follow the screenings. An adult must accompany all children.

WHEN: 1st two Sats in Feb
PARKING: FREE * **THOMAS GUIDE:** 673 E2
KID-FRIENDLY * **WHEELCHAIR/STROLLER ACCESS**

MARCH

Acura LA Bike Tour

START/FINISH LINE AT USC
3551 University Ave, LA 90007
310-444-5544
www.acuralabiketour.com

Watch Lance Armstrong look-alikes and other competitive cyclists spin their wheels through traffic-free LA streets during the nation's biggest cycling event, which starts just hours before the LA Marathon. Celebrity cyclists gear up the 15,000 competitors at the start of their 20-mile marathon. All the streets are closed to vehicles so you have a freewheeling ride through every traffic light and stop sign! REI provides FREE bike safety checks before the event and mobile bike techs ride the route and offer FREE on-course technical assistance. Fee required for the race; no event day registration.

WHEN: 1st Sun in Mar
PARKING: Pay lots ✱ **THOMAS GUIDE:** 634 D5

International Day of the Seal

MARINE MAMMAL CARE CENTER AT FORT MACARTHUR

3601 S Gaffey St (at Leavenworth Dr), San Pedro 90731

310-548-5677

www.mar3ine.org

Tying in with a global awareness day, the non-profit Marine Mammal Care Center holds an open house. Docents are available to answer questions about this facility that rescues and rehabilitates the ocean's injured. Watch narrated care demonstrations of seals and sea lions, attend educational lectures, get the latest information from marine environmental groups. Activities for kids, fund-raising events and tours for new members of the center's support group, MAR3INE. Note: Event is sometimes held in April.

WHEN: Sun in Mar or Apr
PARKING: FREE lot ∗ **THOMAS GUIDE:** 854 B2
KID-FRIENDLY ∗ **WHEELCHAIR/STROLLER ACCESS**

LA Marathon

Starting Line: 6th and Figueroa Sts, LA 90071

310-444-5544

www.lamarathon.com

Witness thousands of feet pounding the pavement at one of the biggest sporting events West of the Mississippi. For 20 years runners have been racing the 26.2 miles through LA's streets, sweating through neighborhoods such as Miracle Mile, Hancock Park and Koreatown. Cheer the 23,000+ marathoners as they sprint by or join the other spectators at the 10 ethnic entertainment centers located along the course. You'll find FREE cultural crafts, music and dance performances. Course starts at 6th and Figueroa and ends at Flower. Check Web site for street closures and most current parking info.

WHEN: 1st Sun in Mar
PARKING: Select downtown lots at reduced fees, about $5 per car
THOMAS GUIDE: 634 E4

LA Marathon Finish Line Festival

Flower and 3rd Streets, LA 90071
310-444-5544
www.lamarathon.com

Greet your sweet and sweaty friends and family who ran all those hot and hilly LA miles at this post-race reunion site. Since spectators are kept from the finish line for security reasons, The Gas Company-sponsored festival area is the place where runners reunite with their supporters. More than 100,000 people gather here to enjoy to FREE entertainment while they wait. It's also the place for runners and walkers to get medical aid and a massage. Food and drinks for sale.

WHEN: 1st Sun in Mar
PARKING: Pay lots east of marathon ✳ **THOMAS GUIDE:** 634 E3
KID-FRIENDLY ✳ **WHEELCHAIR/STROLLER ACCESS**

Nature's Treasures Show

KEN MILLER RECREATION CENTER
3341 Torrance Blvd, Torrance 90503
310-781-7150 (Recreation Center)
www.palosverdes.com/sblap

Gaze at an amazing array of glittering rocks and minerals from around the world at this gem of an event. For more than 50 years the South Bay Lapidary and Mineral Society has been hosting this family-friendly show. The Fluorescent Mineral Society often brings its radiating rock displays that glow under ultraviolet lights. Learn how to carve gems, make glass beads and cut cabochons. Special workshops for kids. Slabs, rough and tumbled stones available for a modest price; gift shop features finished jewelry and lapidary items.

WHEN: Weekend in Mar or Apr
PARKING: FREE * **THOMAS GUIDE:** 763 E5
KID-FRIENDLY * **WHEELCHAIR/STROLLER ACCESS**

St. Patrick's Day LA

DOWNTOWN LA
Flower & 4th Sts, LA 90071
310-537-4240
www.stpatricksdayla.com

Experience LA the Irish way at downtown's processional tribute to the Emerald Isle. Green won't be the only color you see marching in the parade that starts on Flower and 4th Streets. There will be plenty of blue as hundreds of uniformed LA police officers show their civic and Celtic pride by parading on foot, on horses and on motorcycles. LA firefighters join in with dozens of fire department vehicles. Rounding out the hour-long procession are Irish civic groups, Gaelic entertainers and Irish musicians.

WHEN: St. Patrick's Day, March 17
PARKING: Pay lots, metered streets * **THOMAS GUIDE:** 634 E4
KID-FRIENDLY * **WHEELCHAIR/STROLLER ACCESS**

South Bay St. Patrick's Day Parade & Festival

Pier Ave & Valley Dr, Hermosa Beach 90254
310-374-1365
www.stpatricksday.org

Turn green with Celtic pride at one of So Cal's biggest St. Patrick's Day events. An Irish band of merrymakers kicks off the two-day beach town affair with a parade of bag-pipers, drill teams and floats. The procession starts at the City Hall Complex, marches west down Pier Avenue then south on Hermosa where it disbands at Eighth Street. Prepare for mystic merriment at the two-day festival that follows at Pier Plaza. Look for Queen Medb's Encampment with Ancient Celtic Warriors, Irish Setters and Irish Wolfhounds. Live entertainment includes Irish bands and traditional Irish dancers. Bring cash for the carnival rides and the vendors selling Gaelic gifts. Eighty percent of the festival profits supports children's charities in the South Bay and Ireland.

WHEN: Parade, Sat before or on Mar 17; Festival, Sat – Sun
PARKING: FREE with FREE shuttle at Mira Costa High School, 701 S Peck Ave, Manhattan Beach (TG: 762 J1)
THOMAS GUIDE: 762 H2
KID-FRIENDLY * **WHEELCHAIR/STROLLER ACCESS**

Southern California Regional Robotics Competition

LA SPORTS ARENA
3939 S Figueroa St, LA 90037
213-748-6136 (Sports Arena)
www.scrrf.org

Rumble into So Cal's biggest, baddest robotics competi-tion. Robots designed by teams of 2,000 students from 59 US high schools battle each other in this two-day regional competition—one of 23 in the nation—to determine who goes on to the national championship. Each team is given the same kit of parts provided by the mentoring group, FIRST, For Inspiration and Recognition of Science and Technology (www.usfirst.org). Teams have six weeks to design and build their creations. Seeding matches start at 9:30AM, final rounds the second afternoon. If you can't see the largest high school robotics competition in person, check out NASA's Web cast or NASA's cable channel.

WHEN: Last Fri – Sat in Mar
PARKING: Metered street, pay public lots $6+ * **THOMAS GUIDE:** 674 B2
KID-FRIENDLY

Quality of Life Expo

LA CONVENTION CENTER
1201 S Figueroa St, LA 90015
213-741-1151 (Convention Center)
310-444-5544 (Marathon Office)
www.lamarathon.com

What's your exercise quotient? Tune up your workout and tone up for the next LA Marathon and Acura LA Bike Tour at this fitness forum energized with 400 exhibitors and 80,000 buff-it up buffs, marathoners and healthy hopefuls. Dubbed the world's largest Marathon Expo, the event also serves as the pick-up location for all marathon and bike tour participants' essentials. While expo admission is FREE, the parking fee packs a punch.

WHEN: Thu – Sat before LA Marathon (1st Sun in Mar)
PARKING: $10 * **THOMAS GUIDE:** 634 D5
WHEELCHAIR/STROLLER ACCESS

Whale of a Day

POINT VICENTE INTERPRETIVE CENTER
31501 Palos Verdes Dr, Rancho Palos Verdes 90275
310-377-5370
www.palosverdes.com/rpv/recreationparks/

Have a whale of a time at this 20-year-old celebration of the annual Pacific Gray Whale migration from Alaska to Baja, Mexico. The fest location is one of the best places to watch the whales surf the California South Bay (Dec – Apr) on their move from the icy cold north to warm southern lagoons where they give birth. Los Serenos de Point Vicente docents help visitors spot the majestic mammals. FREE children's crafts, storytelling and games. Several marine environmental groups attend including the Long Beach Aquarium, Cabrillo Marine Museum, Marine Mammal Care Center, Whale Watch, South Bay Wildlife Rehab and Palos Verdes Peninsula Land Conservancy.

WHEN: 1st Sat in Mar
PARKING: FREE at Long Point; FREE shuttle ⋆ **THOMAS GUIDE:** 822 F4
KID-FRIENDLY ⋆ **HISTORIC**

Wistaria Festival

MEMORIAL PARK
222 W Sierra Madre Blvd, Sierra Madre 91024
626-306-1150
www.sierramadrewistariafestival.com

It's in the Guinness Book of Records. Sierra Madre's wistaria vine is the world's largest blossoming plant. Purchased in a gallon can for a paltry 75 cents, a local resident planted it in front of his home in 1894. Bad move. By 1930 the vine had overtaken the house, causing the structure to be demolished. Every year the town celebrates the little home wrecker by putting on a festival. Artists display their goods on every available inch of Memorial Park. The city closes off a two-block stretch of Sierra Madre Blvd to house even more artists, plus numerous food stalls and musicians. Ironically, you have to buy timed tickets (includes shuttle ride) to see the actual wistaria vine, which weighs 250 tons and spreads over 2.5 acres. Buy tickets weeks in advance.

WHEN: Sun in Mar, date varies
PARKING: FREE on city streets ⋆ **THOMAS GUIDE:** 567 A2
KID-FRIENDLY ⋆ **HISTORIC** ⋆ **WHEELCHAIR/STROLLER ACCESS**

APRIL

Blessing of the Animals

**EL PUEBLO DE LOS ANGELES
HISTORIC MONUMENT**

125 Paseo de la Plaza (Olvera Street), LA 90012

213-625-5045

www.olvera-street.com

Bestow blessings on your animals at a centuries-old tradition held at LA's most colorful marketplace since 1930. Dress your canines, felines and fowl in their finest and join the procession through Olvera Street led by a flower-decorated cow. The Cardinal of the local Catholic Archdiocese says a benediction and sprinkles Holy Water on the animals as they parade by. Held the Saturday afternoon before Easter (Sabado de Gloria). Note: sometimes held in March depending on where Easter falls in the calendar that year.

WHEN: Sat afternoon before Easter
PARKING: Metered street, pay public lots ★ **THOMAS GUIDE:** 634 G3
KID-FRIENDLY ★ **HISTORIC** ★ **WHEELCHAIR/STROLLER ACCESS**

Blooming of the Roses Festival

EXPOSITION PARK
701 State Drive, LA 90037
213-746-0114 (Hotline)
www.laparks.org

Sprout a new family tradition by attending this weekend fest where everything's coming up roses—9,000 blooming bushes—in the historic Exposition Park Rose Garden. Kids create FREE floral crafts while adults learn rose pruning and garden design in FREE workshops sponsored by the Figueroa Corridor Partnership Business Improvement District and the FREE-admission California Science Center. Discover butterflies and more with FREE family programs included with Natural History Museum paid admission. Take a FREE Rose Garden tour or pay to tour private residential gardens in the historic West Adams District.

WHEN: Last Sat – Sun in Apr
PARKING: Metered street; $5 to $6 lots * **THOMAS GUIDE:** 674 B2
KID-FRIENDLY * **HISTORIC** * **WHEELCHAIR/STROLLER ACCESS**

Cherry Blossom Festival #1

BARNES PARK
350 S McPherrin Ave, Monterey Park 91754
626-307-2541
www.mpkrecreation.com

Experience the sounds, sights and tastes of Japanese culture at this weekend fest. Listen to the rhythms of the *taiko* drums, watch martial artists perform *judo* and *karate,* participate in *ogasawara sencha,* a traditional tea ceremony. Enjoy a *kimono* fashion show, a *hula* dance and a Japanese folk tale puppet performance. Discover the arts of *origami,* hand-made dolls called *kimekomi* and beautiful *bonsai.*

WHEN: 3rd Sat – Sun in Apr
PARKING: FREE at local elementary schools: El Repetto, 650 Gandridge Ave; Ynez, 120 S Ynez; FREE shuttle
THOMAS GUIDE: 636 B2 * **KID-FRIENDLY** * **WHEELCHAIR/STROLLER ACCESS**

Cherry Blossom Festival #2

VICTORY PARK
2575 Paloma St, Pasadena 91107
www.pasadenacherryblossom.org

Japanophiles rejoice and delight in a weekend of culture, entertainment and beauty. Designed to expose mainstream visitors to new, cross-cultural experiences, it offers food, fashion, and fun. Included are Polynesian and Hawaiian dancers, a martial arts arena, vendors, food booths, cultural demonstrations and exhibits. Cherry blossoms symbolize spring, and while the festival celebrates the Japanese experience it also donates 100 cherry trees to Pasadena until 1,000 trees are planted in parks and public places.

WHEN: 1st Sat – Sun in Apr
PARKING: FREE * **THOMAS GUIDE:** 566 E3
KID-FRIENDLY * **WHEELCHAIR/STROLLER ACCESS**

Family Kite Festival

MANHATTAN COUNTY BEACH
12th & 13th Sts, Manhattan Beach 90266
310-802-5419
www.ci.manhattan-beach.ca.us

Go fly a kite on the beach and compete for prizes. Try out for the highest flight, the most attractive kite, the most imaginative kite and the best self-made kite. Learn how to make the famous "Sinbad" kite, a City of Manhattan Beach Parks and Recreation Department favorite. Made out of rice paper, bamboo rods and masking tape, the kite supplies and instructions are FREE. Fly high rain or shine at the end of 12th and 13th Streets, near the Manhattan Beach Pier.

WHEN: Last Sun in Apr
PARKING: Metered beach lots * **THOMAS GUIDE:** 732 F6
KID-FRIENDLY * **WHEELCHAIR/STROLLER ACCESS**

Feria de Los Niños

HOLLENBECK PARK
415 S Saint Louis St, LA 90033
323-261-0113
www.laparks.org

Welcome to Boyle Heights, one of LA's older neighborhoods that celebrates its younger residents—*Los Niños*—with a festival. Rich in Hispanic culture, the 30-year-old fest provides a multitude of cultural activities including a tortilla-making contest, rides across Hollenbeck Lake in flower-decorated Xochimilco boats and Mexican folk tale puppet shows. Spin *Ojo de Dios* (Eye of God) crafts, view the *luminarias* on the lake and play in the Family Sports and Fun Zone.

WHEN: Sat – Sun in Apr, dates vary
PARKING: FREE * **THOMAS GUIDE:** 635 A5
KID-FRIENDLY * **WHEELCHAIR/STROLLER ACCESS**

Garifuna Day Street Festival

Avalon Blvd between 41st & 43rd LA 90011
www.geminaction.com

Celebrate a rare ethnic heritage—Garifuna, a group of a half-million or so people, who hail from the Caribbean Island nations and are a mix of Carib Indians, escaped

African slaves and European ancestry. Occupying three city blocks, the festival celebrates the survival of the Garifuna —who were exiled from their homeland—with traditional music, dance and food. Be sure to try the cassava bread, fried plantains and coconut rice (for a fee). LA recently sanctioned April 12 as the official Garifuna Day.

WHEN: Sat on or before Apr 12
PARKING: FREE * **THOMAS GUIDE:** 674 D3
KID-FRIENDLY * **WHEELCHAIR/STROLLER ACCESS**

LA Times Festival of Books

UCLA
405 Hilgard Ave, LA 90095
800-LA-TIMES x7BOOK
www.latimes.com

Get the buzz on books at the largest biblio fest in the West. About 140,000 literature   lovers come to this two-day book blast to schmooze with 400+ top name authors and score their autographs. Listen to panels on writing and publishing, scoop up bargain books and buy the latest titles from 300+ exhibitors. Several children's entertainment areas bring books to life. Kids can roll with School House Rock, boogey with Barney and be Reading by 9. While admission to the 100+ panels, workshops and author talks is FREE, tickets must be reserved in advance. Tickets available only through Ticketmaster starting the weekend before the event; a few tickets may be available at the fest. Look for a complete festival guide published in the Times the Sunday before.

WHEN: Last Sat – Sun in Apr
PARKING: Campus lots $7 * **THOMAS GUIDE:** 632 B1
KID-FRIENDLY * **WHEELCHAIR/STROLLER ACCESS**

Poppy Day Open House

THEODORE PAYNE FOUNDATION
10459 Tuxford St, Sun Valley 91352
818-768-1802
www.theodorepayne.org

Pop over to this non-profit native plant nursery and get the buzz on what's blooming. Held during the peak of the California poppy season, this open house offers FREE plant talks and propagation demonstrations so local gardeners can populate their properties with the perfect botanicals. Explore the nursery and tour the garden for FREE. Plenty of native plants, seeds and books for sale.

WHEN: 3rd Sat in Apr
PARKING: FREE * **THOMAS GUIDE:** 503 B7
KID-FRIENDLY * WHEELCHAIR/STROLLER ACCESS

Wildflower Show & Plant Sale

MICHAEL LANDON RECREATION CENTER
Malibu Bluffs Park
24250 Pacific Coast Hwy, Malibu 90265
818-881-3706
www.lacnps.org

Go wild at this two-day floral fest promoting botanical beauties native to the Golden State. Walk the walks as California Native Plant Society docents talk the talks along the bluff's paths. Learn how to beautify your own landscape with local flowers and plants. Join the society and get a FREE gift. Garden items, books and posters for sale.

WHEN: Sat – Sun in Apr, dates vary
PARKING: FREE
THOMAS GUIDE: 628 H7
KID-FRIENDLY
WHEELCHAIR/STROLLER ACCESS

Note
FIND FREE EARTH DAY EVENTS UNDER HOLIDAYS

Affaire in the Gardens Art Show

BEVERLY GARDENS PARK
Santa Monica Blvd, Beverly Hills 90210
310-550-4796
www.beverlyhills.org

Attend one of most celebrated art events in the West. More than 225 artists showcase their work on the grassy, glossy landscape of Beverly Hills' popular park, stretching along Santa Monica Blvd between Rodeo and Rexford Drives. The semi-annual weekend art show attracts 40,000 art lovers who come to see and buy the paintings, sculptures, ceramics, jewelry, photos and prints. Kids flex their creativity in the family arts area. FREE on-stage musical entertainment. The affaire returns for a second showing in October.

WHEN: 3rd Sat – Sun in May & Oct
PARKING: Metered city lots off Santa Monica Blvd
THOMAS GUIDE: 592 G7
KID-FRIENDLY ★ **WHEELCHAIR/STROLLER ACCESS**

Calabasas Arts Festival

CALABASAS COMMONS SHOPPING CENTER

Calabasas Rd at Parkway Calabasas, Calabasas 91302

818-878-4242 x270

www.cityofcalabasas.com

View the artistic talents of 200+ local and visiting artists and craftsmen including paintings, pottery, ceramics, sculpture, glass products, jewelry, photography and knit goods. While you browse, enjoy non-stop entertainment from area musicians, singers and dancers. Kids delight in the antics of the costumed fantasy characters that accompany some of the booths, which, in past years, have included a human-size dragonfly on 10-foot stilts and a colorful friendly dragon. Refreshments are available for purchase in the beer & wine garden in the heart of the festival grounds next to Calabasas Commons.

WHEN: 1st Sat – Sun in May
PARKING: FREE lot and street * **THOMAS GUIDE:** 559 E5
KID-FRIENDLY * **WHEELCHAIR/STROLLER ACCESS**

Country Garden Fair

SEPULVEDA GARDEN CENTER

16633 Magnolia Blvd, Encino 91436

888-LA-PARKS

www.laparks.org

Celebrate horticulture at the Sepulveda Dam Recreation Area's 16-acre community garden. The two-day event takes place at the start of the summer growing season, just in time for green thumbs to get cultivation tips on everything from azaleas to zucchini. Tour some of the 800 garden plots, meet local garden club and plant society members and see a bonsai exhibit. Plenty of plants, seeds and country crafts for sale. Bring the kids on Saturday for a petting zoo, music and more. Sponsored by City of LA Department of Recreation and Parks.

WHEN: 3rd Sat – Sun in May
PARKING: FREE ＊ **THOMAS GUIDE:** 561 D3
KID-FRIENDLY ＊ **WHEELCHAIR/STROLLER ACCESS**

Family FunFest

JAPANESE AMERICAN CULTURAL AND COMMUNITY CENTER
244 South San Pedro St, LA 90012
213-628-2725
www.jaccc.org

Take time out to honor your family at Little Tokyo's multicultural weekend fest. On Saturday, celebrate the contemporary Japanese-American holiday, *Kodomo no Hi*, "Children's Day." Once known as "Boy's Day," the traditional Japanese celebration now embraces all children and families. Listen to *taiko* (Japanese drums) performers and participate in drumming sessions. Discover the art of origami, papermaking and calligraphy. On Sunday, the community center celebrates mothers—Hawaiian style-with *mele* (song) groups and *hula* dancers. Learn how to weave *leihulu* (feathers) and *lauhala* (pandandus leaves) then create *ahahui* (fresh flower) and *la'i* (tea leaf) *leis*.

WHEN: 2nd Sat – Sun in May
PARKING: Pay lots ＊ **THOMAS GUIDE:** 634 G5
KID-FRIENDLY ＊ **WHEELCHAIR/STROLLER ACCESS**

Fiesta Hermosa

DOWNTOWN HERMOSA BEACH
Hermosa and Pier Aves, Hermosa Beach 90254
310-376-0951
www.fiestahermosa.com

Fire up your feet and head to the cool waves at this Memorial Weekend beach blast. It's fiesta time and the beach has the throngs and thongs to prove it. A world-class arts & crafts festival with 300+ vendors, shop for handcrafted jewelry, mosaics and one-of-a-kind clothing pieces. Boogie to the beat of live music from the beach-front stage. A second stage pulsates at the beer & wine garden where you can tap into local microbrews. Kids whoop it up on ponies and carnival rides, for a fee. The summer jumpstarting party also reappears as a summer ender around Labor Day Weekend. There's no beach parking available; instead park several blocks away at designated lots. FREE shuttle service.

WHEN: Memorial & Labor Day weekends
PARKING: Northrop Grumman R-5 lot at Manhattan Beach Blvd & Doolittle Dr, Redondo Beach (TG: 733 A5); Mira Costa High School, 701 S Peck Ave, Manhattan Beach (TG: 762 J1)
THOMAS GUIDE: 762 F1
KID-FRIENDLY

Great Los Angeles River Clean Up

FRIENDS OF THE LOS ANGELES RIVER
570 W Ave 26 #250, LA 90065
323-223-0585
www.folar.org

Pull on a pair of work gloves and sturdy shoes and prepare for the one of the biggest environmental clean up operations – La Gran Limpieza. Join 2,000 other volunteers as the non-profit Friends of the Los Angeles River (FoLAR) clears 25 tons of debris from the 52-mile concrete waterway. Choose from 10 cleanup sites along the river from the San Fernando Valley to Long Beach, including the Tujunga Wash, Los Feliz and the Goldenshore Wetlands. By volunteering, you'll learn about this tremendous water resource, meet new friends and create a better LA. And, if you're one of the first 100 volunteers at each station, you'll get a FREE T-shirt.

WHEN: May weekend, date varies, subject to rain delay
PARKING: Call for info * **THOMAS GUIDE:** 594 J6

Jet Propulsion Laboratory's Open House

JET PROPULSION LABORATORY
4800 Oak Grove Dr, Pasadena 91103
818-354-0112
www.jpl.nasa.gov

Rove over space buffs, to the home of the Mars Exploration Rovers. Get in touch with the universe and schmooze with space scientists and engineers. Ask questions about JPL and NASA missions, space communications and the future of galactic technology. Have your picture taken next to a mock-up of a golf-cart sized rover, check out the space flight operations facility and discover what's really underneath an astronaut's spacesuit. Watch an android arm flex its fingers, see test drives of robotic vehicles and touch an iron meteorite. Kids participate in special hands-on activities such making a simple and safe mini-rocket. No backpacks or ice chests allowed. FREE shuttles from parking facilities. Note: Sometimes held in April or June.

WHEN: Weekend, date varies
PARKING: Near Oak Grove main gate
and the lot at Windsor and Arroyo Blvd
THOMAS GUIDE: 535 E5
KID-FRIENDLY * **HISTORIC** * **WHEELCHAIR/STROLLER ACCESS**

LA Harbor Tours

800-831-PORT (tour info available in April)
www.portoflosangeles.org

Cruise the nation's busiest harbor on one-hour narrated boat tours sponsored by the Port of Los Angeles. Offered the third weekend in May in celebration of World Trade Week, the tours leave berths in San Pedro and Wilmington. No reservations are required but expect to wait in line with thousands of other visitors. The open-air tour boats leave every 20 to 60 minutes depending on the location. At least one boat at each departure point is wheelchair accessible; go to the front of line as wheelchair visitors are boarded first. Strollers must be left at the gangway. Bon Voyage!

PORTS O' CALL VILLAGE
Harbor Blvd & 6th St, San Pedro 90731
PARKING: FREE
THOMAS GUIDE: 824 D6

BANNING'S LANDING
100 E Water St, Wilmington 90744
PARKING: Limited; additional at adjacent College of Oceaneering
THOMAS GUIDE: 824 E1

WHEN: 3rd weekend in May
KID-FRIENDLY * HISTORIC * WHEELCHAIR/STROLLER ACCESS

McClave Veterinary Hospital's Annual Pet Fair

MCCLAVE VETERINARY HOSPITAL
6950 Reseda Blvd, Reseda 91335
818-881-5102

Take paws and the pets that go with them to this frisky FREEbie for canines and felines. During National Pet Week, one of the few veterinary hospitals that offers 24-hour emergency care sponsors this small, but fun and informative pet fair. Pick up a sample of the hottest pet foods on the market then sample a FREE hot dog yourself. If you've got a pooch with personality, enter him in one of the fun contests such as "Barest Buns." Sign up for a FREE pet emergency preparedness class and meet the staff of this caring clinic.

WHEN: 1st or 2nd weekend in May
PARKING: FREE lot * **THOMAS GUIDE:** 530 J5
KID-FRIENDLY * **WHEELCHAIR/STROLLER ACCESS**

Mr. Brand's Birthday

BRAND LIBRARY & ART CENTER
Brand Park
1601 West Mountain St, Glendale 91201
818-548-2051
www.ci.glendale.ca.us

Sing "Happy Birthday!" on the second Saturday in May to Leslie C. Brand, the Glendale millionaire who in 1904 built a castle-liked mansion called El Miradero and in his will bequeathed the arched and domed home to the city of Glendale. Brand died in 1925 but you can visit his and his wife's grave under a pyramid-shaped monument in the gated cemetery on the hill behind their former house. Take a FREE ranger-guided tour of the rarely opened resting place, where the childless couple also buried their pet dogs. The festive event at the mansion turned library and art center includes FREE docent-led tours of the Brand home and FREE slices of birthday cake.

WHEN: 2nd Sat in May
PARKING: FREE * **THOMAS GUIDE:** 534 B7
KID-FRIENDLY (OLDER CHILDREN)

Museums of the Arroyo Day

HERITAGE SQUARE
3800 Homer St, LA 90031
Pasadena Museum of History
470 W Walnut St, Pasadena 91103
213-740-TOUR
www.museumsofthearroyo.com

Tour the five grand museums that stand along the Arroyo Seco in Highland Park and Pasadena for FREE—all on one day. See the Gamble House, Heritage Square, Lummis House & Garden, the Southwest Museum and the Pasadena Museum of History, which includes the 1905 Beaux Arts-style Feynes Mansion and the nearby Finnish Folk Art Museum. Wonder how you can see all five in six hours? Park your car and take the FREE shuttles. One travels between Pasadena and Highland Park with stops at Pasadena Museum of History (across from The Gamble House) and the Lummis Home and Garden. The other shuttle moves between the Lummis site, Southwest Museum and Heritage Square. In addition to FREE tours, MOTA Day offers special activities at each stop including period demonstrations, craft workshops and music performances.

WHEN: 3rd Sun in May
PARKING: FREE museum lots and street;
Avery Dennison lot on Walnut St near Pasadena Museum of History
THOMAS GUIDE: 595 B5 & 565 G4
KID-FRIENDLY

NoHo Theatre & Arts Festival

5200 Lankershim Blvd, North Hollywood 91601
818-623-7171
www.nohoartsdistrict.com

Packed with play performances, music stages, storytelling sessions and 50,000 people, this festival is both diverse and crowded. Keep busy for hours with the 75+ live theatre presentations from improv to magic. Children are courted here with a Kids Kourt that showcases local young talent and professional troupes plus an interactive arts & crafts pavilion where professional artists assist kids with tile decorating, mask making and face painting. Parking is a pain; best advice is to park elsewhere and take the Metro Red Line to the North Hollywood Station, where the festivities begin at the entrance.

WHEN: Weekend in May, date varies
PARKING: Very limited; try North Hollywood Park lot @ Magnolia Blvd and Tujunga Ave
THOMAS GUIDE: 562 J2
KID-FRIENDLY * **WHEELCHAIR/STROLLER ACCESS**

Old Pasadena Summer Fest

BROOKSIDE PARK
360 N Arroyo Blvd, Pasadena 91103
626-797-0421
www.OldPasadenaSummerFest.com

Desperately seeking entertainment? Get on over to the San Gabriel Valley's second largest FREE event. Between the Summer Art Fest, Family Fun Fest, Taste of Summer, The Sport Zone and Playboy Jazz in Brookside Park this three-day weekend's got you covered. FREE admission, FREE concerts, FREE hands on art activities for children. The daily hot jazz is a FREEbie courtesy of the Playboy Jazz Festival. Discover 100+ unique California artists displaying and selling hand-blown glass, wooden toys and jeweled jewelry. Splurge on rides for the kids or interactive sports games for adults, too.

WHEN: Memorial Weekend
PARKING: Plenty of parking, check Web site or call for more info
THOMAS GUIDE: 565 F4
KID-FRIENDLY * **WHEELCHAIR/STROLLER ACCESS**

Santa Monica Festival

CLOVER PARK
2600 Ocean Park Blvd, Santa Monica 90405
310-458-8350
www.arts.santa-monica.org

Surf to the seaside city's celebration of its rich environmental and cultural heritage. Emphasizing ecological themes in music, art, education and food, the fest highlights Santa Monica's dedication to environmental education. Learn about energy and water conservation, waste management and chemical usage in exhibitions by the Coalition for Clean Air, Sustainability Works, Heal the Bay and others. Santa Monica K-12 students and faculty teach and entertain with dance, drama and martial arts. Children can create art inspired by world cultures while The Marketplace displays arts & crafts from the Westside and around the world. Go global at the food court that features organic fare.

WHEN: Sat in May, date varies
PARKING: FREE on 28th St south of Ocean Park Blvd
THOMAS GUIDE: 671 J-2
KID-FRIENDLY

Spring Arts Festival

EAGLE ROCK COMMUNITY CULTURAL CENTER
2225 Colorado Blvd, Eagle Rock 90041
323-226-1617
www.erccc.org

Cast your eyes on innovative art inspired by LA-area artists and craftspeople at this Northeast Valley event. Held at the corners of Colorado Blvd. and Caspar St., the outdoor fest features artist displays and demonstrations, children's crafts and live music. The Cultural Center usually hosts a FREE special exhibit in its gallery space, too. Take a close look at the center's building—it's a circa 1914 Carnegie Library listed on the National Registry of Historic Places.

WHEN: Sat in May, date varies
PARKING: Call * **THOMAS GUIDE:** 564 H5
KID-FRIENDLY * **HISTORIC** * **WHEELCHAIR/STROLLER ACCESS**

Taste of the Bowl

HOLLYWOOD BOWL
2301 North Highland Ave, Hollywood 90028
323-850-2000
www.hollywoodbowl.com

Get a jump on the new Hollywood Bowl season with a day-long festival of music and food. The Bowl celebrates opening day of its box office with conducting contests, live music, tours, music workshops, and art projects. Bowl newcomers can learn about summer programs, parking, public transportation, dining, and seating. FREE docent-led tours of the Hollywood Bowl Museum. FREE food tasting stations offer a variety of cuisines. Bowl restaurants also offer full meals or snacks or bring your own food and enjoy a picnic on Bowl grounds.

WHEN: Sat in May, date varies
PARKING: FREE lot * **THOMAS GUIDE:** 593 E4
KID-FRIENDLY * **WHEELCHAIR/STROLLER ACCESS**

Valley Greek Festival

ST. NICHOLAS GREEK ORTHODOX CHURCH
9501 Balboa Blvd, Northridge 91325
818-886-4040

Fill up on sweet, sticky *baklava* at the Valley Greek Festival, a 30+-year tradition at this San Fernando Valley church. While the sweets aren't FREE, general admission is. Immerse yourself in Greek culture, entertainment and ambience at the three-day Memorial Weekend event. More than 50,000 folks turn out to inhale the scents of roasting lamb, Greek sausage and *saganaki* (cheese on fire) and to sample the 14 pastry varieties. The food is irresistible so bring extra cash. For FREE fun, listen to *bouzouki* (mandolin) music, watch traditionally dressed dancers and learn how to cook Greek-style.

WHEN: Memorial Weekend
PARKING: FREE on streets * **THOMAS GUIDE:** 501 C6
KID-FRIENDLY
WHEELCHAIR/STROLLER ACCESS: depends on where you park

Very Special Arts Festival

MUSIC CENTER PLAZA
135 N Grand Ave, LA 90012
213-250-ARTS
www.musiccenter.org/vsaf.html

Rejoice in the artistic talents of local mentally and physically disabled children and witness their joy as they share their creativity with each other, their non-disabled peers, and the community. On display are 1,000+ works of art created by disabled youngsters and their friends. The artworks are based on annual themes such as My California, The Living Ocean and Safari. Children present brief dance, music, and theater performances on two stages throughout the festival. Local museums display and discuss Internet arts programs. Art workshops, face painting, clowns, and balloons add to the joyous atmosphere.

WHEN: Weekday in May, date varies
PARKING: FREE in Music Center garage * **THOMAS GUIDE:** 634 F3
KID-FRIENDLY * **WHEELCHAIR/STROLLER ACCESS**

Venice Classic Bodybuilding Contest

VENICE BEACH RECREATION CENTER

1800 Ocean Front Walk, Venice 90291

310-399-2775

www.laparks.org

Pump it up at this Memorial Day bodybuilding classic on "Muscle Beach" that attracts top male and female bodybuilders from around the word. The 50 contestants display their sculpted forms and compete under amateur rules vying for "Most Muscular" and "Most Sculpted" prizes. FREE for spectators; fee to compete. In addition to muscle-bound athletes, the beach attracts an offbeat show of flamboyant skaters, skateboarders and performance artists.

WHEN: Memorial Day (Mon)
PARKING: Call * **THOMAS GUIDE:** 671 G6
KID-FRIENDLY * **WHEELCHAIR/STROLLER ACCESS**

Note
FIND FREE CINCO DE MAYO EVENTS UNDER HOLIDAYS
*

Bellflower Boulevard Car Show

Between Pacific Ave & Park St, Bellflower 90706
562-804-1424
www.bellflower.org

Zoom down to downtown Bellflower and custom-car history at this waxed-up, fin-backed, flame-topped Bellflower Boulevard street show. Check out 300+ custom rods, roadsters, classics, trucks and Harleys parked along 2 to 3 blocks of the boulevard. About 10,000 car enthusiasts come out to ogle the artful autos, listen to music and enter the raffle drawings.

WHEN: Sat in June, date varies
PARKING: FREE * **THOMAS GUIDE:** 736 C5
KID-FRIENDLY

Christopher Street West Gay & Lesbian Pride Parade & Festival

SANTA MONICA BLVD
Between Crescent Heights & Robertson Blvds,
West Hollywood 90069
323-969-8302
www.lapride.org

Jump over the rainbow and join one of the country's largest pride parades and festivals. West Hollywood puts on a powerful three-day show of pride for its largely gay & lesbian community. The Sunday parade is FREE; the West Hollywood Park festival costs admission each day. Join 350,000 spectators as the procession wades through the throngs along Santa Monica Blvd. from Crescent Heights to Robertson. Filled with floats of flamboyant folks, the parade also features groups of gay seniors, parents of gays, and both gay and heterosexual celebs, politicians, police and firefighters. Grand Marshals have included Cyndi Lauper and Gilbert Baker, creator of the famous rainbow flag. Parking in the already crowded city is crazy but at least parking permit restrictions are lifted for the massive event.

WHEN: Fri — Sun in June, dates vary; parade always on Sun
PARKING: Metered street, pay lots * **THOMAS GUIDE:** 593 H7 to 593 B6
KID-FRIENDLY * **WHEELCHAIR/STROLLER ACCESS**

Concours on Rodeo

RODEO DRIVE
Between Wilshire and Santa Monica Blvds, Beverly Hills 90212
1-800-345-2210
www.beverlyhillsbehere.org

See a century of automotive history along with 100+ of the fastest, sleekest and rarest collector cars on famous Rodeo Drive. Held on Father's Day, the Beverly Hills exhibition displays cars dating from the two-cylinder 1901 Panhard et Levassor through a present day Ferrari that goes from zero to 60 in under four seconds and sells for nearly $700,000. Hot rods, Woodys, classic convertibles, muscle cars, and great European classics are on view as well as cars from collections of the rich and famous, including frequent exhibitors Jay Leno, Nicholas Cage, and Tim Allen. Some are truly vintage—one of only a handful ever made.

WHEN: Father's Day, 3rd Sun in June
PARKING: Metered street, pay lots * **THOMAS GUIDE:** 632 F1 2

Family Fishing Derby

POLLIWOG POND PARK
1601 Manhattan Beach Blvd, Manhattan Beach 90266
310-802-5419
www.citymb.info

Bring your rod and reel—if you're age 3 to 12—and learn basic fishing techniques in a clinic held by the city Parks & Recreation Department. After practicing casting and reeling in, kids compete in age groups for most fish, longest fish and the most interesting catch. All caught fish are released back into the pond. Children under age 6 must be accompanied by an adult. Bring a sack lunch because all that fishing will make you hungry!

WHEN: Sat in June, date varies
PARKING: FREE * **THOMAS GUIDE:** 732 H6
KID-FRIENDLY * **WHEELCHAIR/STROLLER ACCESS**

Fiesta of Gems Show

VETERANS MEMORIAL AUDITORIUM
4117 Overland Ave, Culver City 90232
310-253-6630
www.gembiz.com

Rock at an event tumbling with…rocks. And minerals, gems, smooth stones, fossils, and jewelry. Sponsored by the Culver City Rock and Mineral Club, Inc., the club and its event have been rockin' for 40+ years. Gaze at 50 exhibit cases stocked with glittering displays. Watch as craftsmen demonstrate the arts of gem carving, cabochon-making and faceting. Junior rock hounds receive FREE gift specimens.

WHEN: Sat – Sun in June, dates vary
PARKING: FREE * **THOMAS GUIDE:** 672 G2
KID-FRIENDLY * **WHEELCHAIR/STROLLER ACCESS**

It's a SoRo World Festival

SOUTH ROBERTSON BLVD
Between Pico Blvd & Airdrome St, LA 90035
310-836-7979
www.soro.org

Tango at "a rainbow of music and dance" as the South Robertson Neighborhoods Council sponsors this summer street scene. The ethnically diverse area north of the 10 Freeway and south of Beverly Hills celebrates its heritages with live performances, arts & crafts and international cuisine. Take advantage of the FREE afternoon tango lessons offered on the dance floor. Kids keep busy at Camp SoRo at Hamilton High School with a moon bounce, inflatable slide and crafts.

WHEN: Sun in June, date varies
PARKING: Metered street, pay lots * **THOMAS GUIDE:** 632 J4
KID-FRIENDLY

Juneteenth Celebration

WILLIAM GRANT STILL ARTS CENTER

2520 S West View, LA 90016

323-857-7000

www.fowgs.org

Learn about the African Diaspora, discover current Afro-American culture and discuss the future of Black America on Juneteenth. The day commemorates the reading of the Emancipation Proclamation to Texas slaves on June 19, 1865—2 ½ years after President Lincoln penned the document. Celebrate with the Friends of William Grant Still Arts Center—named for the Black American composer. Listen to FREE gospel music at the Metropolitan AME Zion church across the street and jazz, pop, salsa, reggae, and blues at the center's main stage. View a new gallery exhibit highlighting local Black artists and browse vendors selling clothing, candles and hand-made jewelry. Join the round-table discussions and feast on the food court's American, African and Caribbean cuisine. A Youth Village offers FREE face painting, storytelling, doll making, geography games, youth performing groups and a jumping machine.

WHEN: Sat on or before June 19

PARKING: FREE * **THOMAS GUIDE:** 633 D6

KID-FRIENDLY * **HISTORIC** * **WHEELCHAIR/STROLLER ACCESS**

Juneteenth Jubilee

MARTIN LUTHER KING, JR. PARK

1950 Lemon Ave, Long Beach 90806

562-570-4405

www.ci.long-beach.ca.us/park/

Join the jubilant vibe at Juneteenth; a day commemorating the Union Army's reading of the Emancipation Proclamation to Galveston, Texas slaves on June 19, 1865 —2 ½ years after President Lincoln issued the document.

On this day they learned the Civil War was over and that they were free. An official holiday in the Lone Star state, Juneteenth is gaining momentum in the rest of the US as a celebration of African-American culture. The local daylong festival of music for the soul and soul food features picnic-style family games such as tug-of-war plus community booths and community spirit.

WHEN: Sat on or before June 19
PARKING: FREE * **THOMAS GUIDE:** 795 F4
KID-FRIENDLY * **HISTORIC** * **WHEELCHAIR/STROLLER ACCESS**

LA Kids Read Festival

LOS ANGELES CENTRAL LIBRARY
630 W 5th St, LA 90071
213-228-7480
www.lapl.org/kidspath

Instill a love of reading in your children and you'll give them a head start toward a passion for learning and personal growth. Where to begin? This FREE festival at the Central Library! Live music, well-known story characters, face painting, arts and crafts, and FREE prizes are part of this June afternoon devoted to an appreciation of literature. In addition, the Library presents its annual Leader Reader Award to a local celebrity who has demonstrated dedication to the advancement of juvenile literacy.

WHEN: Sat afternoon in early June
PARKING: Pay lots, structures * **THOMAS GUIDE:** 634 E4
KID-FRIENDLY

Montrose Arts & Crafts Festival

MONTROSE SHOPPING PARK

2200-2400 blocks of Honolulu Ave, Montrose 91208

818-248-3889

www.shopmontrose.com

Go retro at this Crescenta Valley shopping area renowned for its tree-lined streets and old-fashioned storefronts. About 30,000 visitors come to reclaim another time while browsing and buying from 300+ juried arts & crafts vendors. Local stores also hold special FREE events such as artisan demonstrations and book signings. Pick a fruitful feast at the popular Harvest Market, a certified farmer's market that stretches along an entire block. The two-day event includes live entertainment, a Kid's Zone and International Food Court.

WHEN: Sat – Sun in June, dates vary
PARKING: FREE * **THOMAS GUIDE:** 534 H4
KID-FRIENDLY * **WHEELCHAIR/STROLLER ACCESS**

Oodles of Noodles Festival

TORRANCE CULTURAL ARTS CENTER

3330 Civic Center Dr, Torrance 90503

310-781-7150

www.tcac.torrnet.com

Slurp oodles of spicy, saucy, sizzling noodles including Japanese *soba,* Chinese *lo mein* and Italian spaghetti at this aptly named fest. FREE cultural workshops such as silk painting, fan and flute making, and traditional Chinese paper cutting. Embracing a wide variety of cultures, the event includes Celtic music, Japanese folk songs and Greek dancing.

WHEN: Weekend in June, date varies
PARKING: FREE * **THOMAS GUIDE:** 763 E5
KID-FRIENDLY * **WHEELCHAIR/STROLLER ACCESS**

Salute to Recreation Family Festival

NORTHRIDGE PARK

10058 Reseda Blvd, Northridge 91324
818-756-8060 or 818-349-0535 day of the event
www.laparks.org

Get your body moving to the San Fernando Valley's largest event. A showcase for the City of LA Recreation and Parks Department, the festival draws about 100,000 people over a three-day weekend. Visit the Hawaiian Village & Stage for some *hula* lessons; watch some hot steps in the salsa dance competition and view artists' visions in the mural competition display. The weekend blast includes fireworks on Saturday, an International Children's Village, carnival games and rides, petting zoo and health fair. Continuous entertainment on four stages. Admission is FREE but rides and other activities require cash.

WHEN: 1st weekend in June
PARKING: Limited FREE in lot, streets * **THOMAS GUIDE:** 500 J5
KID-FRIENDLY * **WHEELCHAIR/STROLLER ACCESS**

Van Nuys Aviation Expo

VAN NUYS AIRPORT

8030 Balboa Blvd, Van Nuys 91406
818-909-3529
www.lawa.org

Book a morning landing at Van Nuys Airport to see vintage aircraft on the ground and state-of-the-art jets in the air. The expo is one of the world's largest and features replicas of famous aircraft (which have included the Wright Bros. biplane and B1 Bombers), flyovers by modern and classic planes, aerobatics performances, hang gliding demonstrations, and skydiving shows. Past shows have featured flight displays of the F-117A Stealth Fighter, F-15E Strike Eagle, and a World War II Corsair fighter. Due to the recent political climate, the military aircraft may not be present. On the ground wing it to interactive aviation-related activities for children, flight-related exhibits and a flight simulator. Concession stands offer food and live music plays all day on the main stage.

WHEN: Sat in June, date varies
PARKING: FREE at CSUN North Campus; LA County Courthouse in Van Nuys; Woodley Golf Course. FREE shuttle. On-site parking for disabled
THOMAS GUIDE: 531 D2

KID-FRIENDLY * WHEELCHAIR/STROLLER ACCESS

JULY

Absolut Chalk

OLD PASADENA
Between Pasadena Ave & Green St, Pasadena 91105
626-440-7370
www.absolutchalk.com

Chalk up the town at the world's largest street painting festival featuring more than 700 artists; many have perfected the European art known as Madonnari. The murals are created over a weekend and draw 40,000 onlookers. While champion chalkers must pre-register for assigned spaces, non-competitors of all ages create their own "street art" in a small area called Chalkland. Be aware that all murals are washed away at festival's end. Sponsored by Absolut, proceeds from the festival benefit its host, the non-profit Light Bringer Project. Usually held in Centennial Square, the fest will happen elsewhere in Old Pasadena due to city hall retrofitting through 2007. Note: Event is sometimes held in June.

WHEN: Sat – Sun in July, dates vary
PARKING: Fee for public lots, metered streets * **THOMAS GUIDE:** 565 J4
KID-FRIENDLY

Central Avenue Jazz Festival

CENTRAL AVENUE
Between 42nd and 43rd Sts, LA 90011
213-473-7700
www.culturela.org

Breeze to "The Avenue" for a two-day block party featuring top jazz musicians, just across the street from LA's hippest historic hotel. Known as the "Jewel of Central Avenue," the Dunbar Hotel was the first first-class hotel for Blacks during a time when African Americans could not stay in white-only establishments. Built in 1928, the hotel guest list included music greats Duke Ellington, Billie Holiday and Cab Calloway. Discover the legendary hotel's history, meet members of the LA Jazz Society and dine on ethnic cuisine. Don't forget to listen to the FREE jazz in an area once known as "Little Harlem West."

WHEN: Sat – Sun in July, dates vary
PARKING: Metered street, pay lots * **THOMAS GUIDE:** 674 F3
KID-FRIENDLY * **WHEELCHAIR/STROLLER ACCESS**

Dragon Boat Races

LONG BEACH MARINE STADIUM
5255 Paoli Way, Long Beach 90803
562-570-8920 (Sea Festival Hotline)
562-570-3100 (Park & Rec Dept)
www.lbparks.org

Feast your eyes on fantastic colorful creatures of the sea, as fire-breathing dragons skirt the waters off Long Beach. The fantasy figures are really outriggers decorated in an age-old Chinese festival tradition. The delightful dragons face off in races during the two-day boating event that's part of the summer-long International Sea Festival (see separate entry this month). The races are FREE for spectators.

WHEN: Date varies
PARKING: FREE around stadium, fee for beach lots
THOMAS GUIDE: 826 C1
KID-FRIENDLY * WHEELCHAIR/STROLLER ACCESS

Glendale Cruise Night Car Show and Street Party

BRAND BOULEVARD
Between Broadway and Doran Sts, Glendale 91203
818-548-6464
www.ci.glendale.ca.us

Slick back your hair or pull on your bobby-socks and cruise to Brand Boulevard for one of the hottest hot rod, custom, classic and restored car shows. Look under the hoods of 400+ pre-1972 cars that line both sides of Brand. About 35,000 car fans attend the nighttime event to chat with '57 T-Bird owners and listen to live entertainment on the Wilson Avenue concert stage. FREE stuff includes a children's activity center and radio station booths with giveaways.

WHEN: Sat eve in July, date varies
PARKING: FREE * **THOMAS GUIDE:** 564 E4
KID-FRIENDLY * WHEELCHAIR/STROLLER ACCESSIBLE

Ho 'olaule 'a (Hawaiian Street Festival)

ALONDRA PARK
3850 W Manhattan Beach Blvd, Lawndale 90260
www.hiccsc.org

Hula hula over to a Polynesian party at this weekend celebration of Hawai'i's multicultural heritage. For FREE fun, hit the cultural booths to learn how to create a *haku lei,* strum a *ukulele* and tell a traditional Hawaiian tale. Watch and listen to live Pacific Islander performances and stroll through arts & crafts booths. Bring cash to taste Hawaiian treats from a *lu`au* plate to *huli huli* chicken and shaved ice.

WHEN: 3rd weekend in July
PARKING: Check Web site ∗ **THOMAS GUIDE:** 733 E6
KID-FRIENDLY ∗ **WHEELCHAIR/STROLLER ACCESS**

International Sea Festival

LONG BEACH MARINE STADIUM
5255 Paoli Way, Long Beach 90803
562-570-8920 (Sea Festival Hotline)
562-570-3100 (Park & Rec Dept)
www.lbparks.org

Swim in summer-long fun during this sea-sational festival that's been around for 70+ years. Dive into more than 15 activities held from early July to late August, many of them FREE! Say Aloha! at the Tiki Beach Festival, cheer on Chinese Dragon Boats as they race across the water, watch sand sculptors create temporary works of art. Kids can float their hand-made boats in a regatta, families can move to the beat of the Long Beach Municipal Band and sports fans can watch everything from speed boat races to beach volleyball tournaments. For specific dates and times and to sign-up to participate in an event, check out the Web site of the Long Beach Department of Parks, Recreation and Marine, which sponsors the festival.

WHEN: July to Aug, dates vary
PARKING: FREE around stadium, fee for beach lots
THOMAS GUIDE: 826 C1
KID-FRIENDLY ∗ **WHEELCHAIR/STROLLER ACCESS**

Kites Over Redondo

REDONDO BEACH PIER
100 W Torrance Blvd, Redondo 90277
310-318-0631 (Pier) 310-372-0308 (Kites)
www.sunshinekiteco.com
www.redondopier.com

Fly high with your deltas, diamonds and sky clippers at Sunshine Kite Co.'s breezy festival. Let the wind guide you to the pier and the site of the company-sponsored fest. For high-tech, rip-stopping, heart-jumping fun, watch the top kite fliers maneuver their powerful sports kites through the air. Don't know how to fly a kite? The company offers FREE flying lessons, whether you buy a kite or bring your own.

WHEN: Sun afternoon, date varies
PARKING: Fee for Pier/Plaza (expensive), metered lots
THOMAS GUIDE: 762 J5
KID-FRIENDLY * WHEELCHAIR/STROLLER ACCESS

LA Kings Development Camp

HEALTH SOUTH TRAINING CENTER
555 Nash St, El Segundo 90245
310-535-4510
www.lakings.com

Spend your summer on ice and see future LA Kings stars before they make headlines. It's two weeks of hockey in July as 30+ Kings' top draft picks and premier hopefuls skate, scrimmage and sweat it out on and off the ice. All on-ice workouts are open to the public, including two practices each day. Get your NHL pre-season fix at the camp's FREE Exhibition game. The end-of-camp evening face-off attracts about 1,000 Kings fans. The FREE tickets are available about 3 hours before game time so line up early. Go Kings!

WHEN: Two weeks in July, dates vary
PARKING: FREE * **THOMAS GUIDE:** 732 H1
KID-FRIENDLY * **WHEELCHAIR/STROLLER ACCESS**

Long Beach Live!

Downtown Long Beach 90802
562-436-4259
www.downtownlongbeach.org

Dive into this new three-day FREE street festival brimming with FREE activities. Divided into four main areas: cuisine, kids, lifestyle and music, the fest is a showcase of Downtown Long Beach's arts & culture and features live performing acts, musicians and street artists. While mingling with the crowd, look for the community's colorful murals and outdoor art—it's everywhere, even on phone booths, and it's FREE!

WHEN: Fri - Sat in July, dates vary
PARKING: Metered street, pay lots * **THOMAS GUIDE:** 825 D & E1
KID-FRIENDLY * **WHEELCHAIR/STROLLER ACCESS**

Lotus Festival

ECHO PARK LAKE
Between Glendale Blvd and Park Ave, LA 90026
213- 485-8743
www.laparks.org

Celebrate Asian and Pacific Islander cultures at the largest Lotus bed in the U.S. In July, water lilies and other lotuses break out in riotous bloom in Echo Park Lake, the site of the two-day event. Packed with activities and entertainment designed to foster an appreciation for Eastern art, music, and lifestyles, the fest draws 150,000 visitors each year. Create Asian-inspired artworks at FREE demonstrations of paper cutting, scroll painting and calligraphy. Cheer on the Chinese Dragon Boat races with contests among local businesses, community leaders and colleges. Look for Queens and princesses garbed in their native traditional attire and community booths stocked with FREE information. Kids gravitate to the FREE Children's Courtyard for arts & crafts, live music and stories. A FREE nighttime fireworks show culminates each day's activities.

WHEN: Sat – Sun in July, dates vary
PARKING: FREE at Logan Street School, 1711 W Montana St;
Echo Park Baseball Diamond 1632 Bellevue Ave;
and City of Angels Medical Center, 1711 W Temple Ave, FREE shuttle
THOMAS GUIDE: 634 E1
KID-FRIENDLY * **WHEELCHAIR/STROLLER ACCESS**

Malibu Arts Festival

MALIBU CIVIC CENTER
23555 Civic Center Way, Malibu 90265
310-456-9025
www.malibu.org/artfestival

Taste the tang of salty sea air and feel the caress of ocean breezes as you peruse the artwork of local and visiting artists. A mid-summer, weekend-long happening just yards away from the Pacific Ocean, the fest features the work of 200+ painters, photographers, sculptors, furniture makers, jewelry artisans, and other artists. Professional and local bands entertain throughout the weekend and a food court features specialties from local restaurants and caterers. The Malibu Optimist Club offers a pancake breakfast for a small charge from 8:30AM to 11AM.

WHEN: Sat – Sun in July, dates vary
PARKING: $4 lot * **THOMAS GUIDE:** 625 J7

San Fernando Valley Obon Festival

JAPANESE AMERICAN COMMUNITY CENTER
12953 Branford St, Pacoima 91311
818-899-1989
www.sfvjacc.org

Honor ancestral spirits at this Japanese Buddhist festival with a 1,400-year-old history. During this time of year Buddhists believe the spirits of dead relatives reunite with their earth-bound relations. Sponsored by the San Fernando Valley Hongwanji Buddhist Temple, the two-day festival features live performances and exhibits of Japanese culture. A highlight is the FREE performance of *odori,* a lively ancient dance that consoles the ghosts. Dancers dress in colorful cotton *kimonos* and white socks using fans to punctuate their steps. Listen to the pounding of *taiko* drums and watch the precision movements of *kendo* (wooden swordsmanship) and *karate* then view the more subdued display of *ikebani* (Japanese flower arrangements).

WHEN: Sat – Sun in July, dates vary
PARKING: Call for more information * **THOMAS GUIDE:** 502 E6
KID-FRIENDLY * **WHEELCHAIR/STROLLER ACCESS**

Shakespeare in the Square

PERSHING SQUARE
532 S Olive Street, LA 90013
213-481-BARD
www.shakespearefestivalla.org

Behold one of the Bard's best plays on an outdoor stage, presented every Tuesday through Sunday for three weeks in July. Bring a blanket, a picnic basket and a canned food donation and enjoy an Elizabethan tale told under the stars for FREE. Shakespeare Festival/LA produces the professional and critically acclaimed al fresco program that has provided $1.5 million worth of food to those in need since it began in 1984. Pay $40 for reserved seating and help the show go on.

WHEN: Tue – Sun, 3 weeks in July, dates vary
PARKING: Metered street, pay lot under the square
THOMAS GUIDE: 634 F4
KID-FRIENDLY * **WHEELCHAIR/STROLLER ACCESS**

South Bay Greek Festival

ST. KATHERINE GREEK ORTHODOX CHURCH
722 Knob Hill, Redondo Beach 90277
310-540-2434
www.sbgreekfestival.com

Dance with zeal and eat lamb with zest when you become Zorba for the weekend at this three-day celebration of everything Greek. The *baklava* is sweet and the *gyros* sizzle at the 40+-year South Bay event oozing with Hellenic tradition. Admission is cheap by any standards: $2 adults, $1 seniors and FREE for ages 12 and under, but older folks can also get in FREE by printing out a FREE-admission coupon from the festival Web site.

WHEN: Fri – Sat in July, dates vary
PARKING: Call for more information * **THOMAS GUIDE:** 762 J7
KID-FRIENDLY * **WHEELCHAIR/STROLLER ACCESS**

Note
**FIND FREE
JULY FOURTH
EVENTS UNDER
HOLIDAYS**
*

Children's Festival of the Arts

DELONGPRE PARK
1350 N Cherokee Ave, Hollywood 90028
323-462-2355
www.hollywoodartscouncil.org

Excite kids about the arts at a FREE fair where they can find and develop a love of artistic and cultural diversity. The Hollywood Arts Council and the Junior Arts Center present this mid-summer festival, which combines exhibitions of storytelling, puppetry, music, and dance. Professional artists lead workshops where youngsters make their own masks, musical instruments, puppets, keepsake books and other projects. The Council brings artists from around the world to expose children to a vast array of artistic expression, including the art of professional Hollywood movie make-up.

WHEN: Sun afternoon in Aug, date varies
PARKING: FREE on Sunset Blvd and Crossroads of the World
(Sunset and Las Palmas) FREE shuttles from several parking areas
in Hollywood (see Web site for details) * **THOMAS GUIDE:** 593 E5
KID-FRIENDLY * **WHEELCHAIR/STROLLER ACCESS**

Courtyard Kids Festival

JAPANESE AMERICAN NATIONAL MUSEUM

369 E First St, LA 90012

213-625-0414

www.janm.org

Come to the museum's Children's Courtyard and enjoy enriching and engaging activities for families based on the Japanese American experience. Participate in art contests, art displays, experiment with *origami.* Listen to traditional storytellers as well as authors of young adult and children's books who read their work, meet with readers and discuss their books. A family-friendly social event, with special activities for toddlers, the fest highlights the Courtyard's permanent installation of stone pavers inscribed with the individual names of children 21 years and younger. Stone paver donations help support the museum's mission of preserving Japanese American heritage.

WHEN: Sun in Aug, date varies

PARKING: Fee * **THOMAS GUIDE:** 634 G4

KID-FRIENDLY * **WHEELCHAIR/STROLLER ACCESS**

Fiesta La Ballona

VETERAN'S PARK

4117 Overland Ave, Culver City 90230

310-253-6639

www.fiestalaballona.org

No, it's not a tribute to luncheon meat. It's a weeklong celebration of the homey, yet sophisticated town of Culver City, which is nestled in the folds of the La Ballona Valley. The Fiesta began in 1951 to honor the Valley's early settlers and has expanded its scope and location beyond its base at Veteran's Park to include music at local night spots, plays at neighborhood theaters, tours of historic downtown, and more than 20 other events. Most of the weekend park events are FREE, including martial arts demonstrations, parades, an outdoor world music concert, and demonstrations by the Culver City Fire and Police Departments. Jewelry, ceramics and leather goods crafted by professional artists and works of art created by local youngsters are on display, too. Many of the off-site happenings charge a fee. Nearby restaurants offer gourmet and down home fare.

WHEN: Week in late Aug, fest on weekend
PARKING: FREE in lot at park and structure on Overland Ave, half block north of Culver Blvd
THOMAS GUIDE: 672 F2
KID-FRIENDLY ∗ **WHEELCHAIR/STROLLER ACCESS**

Fishing Rodeo

BELMONT VETERANS MEMORIAL PIER
Ocean Blvd & 39th Pl., Long Beach 90830
562-570-8920 (Fest hotline)
www.lbparks.org

Drop a line over the pier and try to reel in the big one. Open to kids ages 16 and younger, the International Sea Festival's (see event in July chapter) fishing rodeo has been held for more than 50 years. Armed with poles and tackle and FREE bait, the young anglers compete for the biggest, smallest and most unusual catch of the day. FREE raffle and FREE ice cream and soda for participants. Sponsored by Long Beach Department of Parks & Recreation & Marine and the Southern California Tuna Club.

WHEN: Fri morning in Aug or July, date varies
PARKING: Metered lot ∗ **THOMAS GUIDE:** 825 J2
KID-FRIENDLY ∗ **WHEELCHAIR/STROLLER ACCESS**

Great Sand Sculpture Contest

BELMONT PLAZA OLYMPIC POOL BEACH AREA

4000 Olympic Plaza Dr, Long Beach 90830

562-570-8920 (Fest hotline)

www.lbparks.org

Haul out those pails and shovels and scoop your way to the shore for a beachy competition. Teams of co-workers, families and friends compete against each other to carve unique sand creations under the summer sun. Spectators can watch the artful contestants digging and designing from 9AM until 1:30PM when judging begins. Sand sculptures remain on display until 4PM when either the elements or beach goers dismantle them. FREE to see; entry fee for teams but FREE to youth teams ages 12 and younger.

WHEN: Sat in Aug, date varies
PARKING: Metered lot * **THOMAS GUIDE:** 826 A2
KID-FRIENDLY

International Surf & Health Festival

HERMOSA, MANHATTAN & REDONDO BEACH PIERS

Pier Plaza & Beach Ave, Hermosa Beach 90254

Manhattan Beach Blvd & Ocean Dr, Manhattan Beach 90266

S Catalina Ave & Torrance Blvd, Redondo Beach 90277

310-802-5400

www.surffestival.org

Reel in some slammin' summer fun in the South Bay. Whether you participate in the beach-related sports or just enjoy them from the sidelines, this multi-site festival will keep you in the swim all weekend. The fishing derby and sandcastle-building contest are FREE, but check the Web site for pre-registration requirements. Participation in the surfing competition, beach race, volleyball tournament, pier-to-pier swim race, and youth swim and paddle competitions may require fees and pre-registration. Watch lifeguards give rescue demonstrations and then face off in relay races. See pro surfing and bodysurfing contests. A Health Fair provides screenings and wellness information. Arts & crafts demonstrations and sales all weekend.

Various South Bay venues (check Web site for details)

WHEN: Early Aug, late July
PARKING: Pay lots
THOMAS GUIDE: 762 G2 (Hermosa) 732 F6 (Manhattan)
762 J5 (Redondo)
KID-FRIENDLY

Kids 'n Kritters Day

HARVEST MARKET
Honolulu Ave & Ocean View Blvd, Montrose 91020
818-248-3889
www.shopmontrose.com/harvestmkt

Adopt a puppy, kitten, or stray from the local shelter, enjoy a FREE magic show, or just hang out with the family at this Harvest Market event. Dedicated to the children of La Crescenta Valley and Glendale, the special Sunday event helps promote the hip and homey farmer's market that stretches for a block in the Montrose Shopping Park. Nibble on the vendors' wares as you stroll the boulevard, or grab a table at one of the many restaurants in between the rides and games (may require fee). Take time to smell the flowers and admire the organic produce from these certified California farmers. Tour the FREE Wild Wonders exotic petting zoo featuring millipedes, macaws, hedgehogs and chinchillas.

WHEN: Sun in late Aug
PARKING: FREE * **THOMAS GUIDE:** 534 H3
KID-FRIENDLY * **WHEELCHAIR/STROLLER ACCESS**

Nisei Week

LITTLE TOKYO
San Pedro Street
Between 1st and 3rd Sts, LA 90012
213-687-7193
www.niseiweek.org

Just say "hai" (yes) to this Japanese festival that lasts for two weekends and features several FREE activities and events. Started by second-generation Japanese Americans *(Nisei)* in 1934 during the Great Depression, the festival has endured despite interruptions due to the internment of Japanese during World War II. Revived in 1949, the festival promotes Japanese culture and continues to bring unity to the LA-area Japanese community. Attend the Street Arts Festival held both weekends, browse unique Japanese art for sale and watch the Sushi Academy roll up seaweed and rice. Take in the colorful procession of the Grand Parade on the first Sunday or the beat of the Taiko Drum Gathering both Sundays. Highlights include folk art and *bonsai* exhibits, martial arts demonstrations and tea ceremonies. Don't miss the festival finale—Ondo Street Dancing where spectators can join the *kimono*-clad dancers. Event locations include Japanese American Cultural & Community Center, Japanese Village Plaza, and Japanese American National Museum.

WHEN: 1st and 2nd weekend in Aug
PARKING: Pay lots, metered street ∗ **THOMAS GUIDE:** 634 G4
KID-FRIENDLY ∗ **WHEELCHAIR/STROLLER ACCESS**

Tiki Beach & Polynesian Spectacular

GRANADA LAUNCH RAMP

Granada Ave & Ocean Blvd, Long Beach 90830

562-570-8920 (Fest hotline)

www.lbparks.org

Put on your grass skirt and *lei* then *hula hula* to this big beach bash that starts with a sunrise ceremony and ends at sundown with a *luau*. One of the last beachside events held as part of the summer-long International Sea Festival, the fest is easy to find—just look for the carved Tikis dotting the beach. Tiki party activities include outrigger canoe and catamaran rides, a kite-surfing exhibition and a FREE area for kids. Visit the island marketplace and purchase authentic island foods. If you want to feast at the traditional island luau it will cost you $25 per person.

WHEN: Sat in Aug, date varies
PARKING: Metered lot * **THOMAS GUIDE:** 826 A2
KID-FRIENDLY

Watts Summer Festival

WATTS LABOR COMMUNITY ACTION COMMITTEE CENTER

10950 S Central Ave, Watts 90059

323-789-7304 (Fest hotline)

323-563-5639 (Center)

www.wattsfestival.org

Support unity and racial harmony at the oldest African-American cultural festival in the US. Born out of the ashes of the Watts Riots in 1965, the festival promotes cultural awareness for children and families. Packed with a lineup of music, performing arts presentations, fashion, movie screenings and art & crafts, the FREE festival has drawn top artists such as Stevie Wonder, Isaac Hayes and James Brown. Grand Marshals for the three-day event have included Coretta Scott King, Muhammad Ali and Quincy Jones. The group behind the festival was responsible for the famous "Wattstax" production that spawned a feature film and record album of the same name.

WHEN: Fri — Sat in Aug, date varies
PARKING: Pay lot * **THOMAS GUIDE:** 704 F6
KID-FRIENDLY * **WHEELCHAIR/STROLLER ACCESS**

SEPTEMBER

Abbot Kinney Boulevard Festival

ABBOT KINNEY BOULEVARD
Between Venice Blvd & Main St, Venice 90291
310-396-3772
www.abbotkinney.org

Journey to Venice-of-America and relive the artistic vision of its founder, Abbot Kinney, the man responsible for the community's canals and Venetian architecture. In 1984, the Bohemian boulevard was thoughtfully named after this visionary by the merchants of Venice, also known as the Abbot Kinney District Association. This group of civic-minded shop owners offer a festival packed with FREEbies including live theatre, amusement rides and a petting zoo. If you want to spend cash, more than 300 vendors line the thoroughfare between Venice Blvd and Main St while the renowned restaurants on "The Street" offer a "Taste of Venice."

WHEN: Sun in late Sept
PARKING: Fee * **THOMAS GUIDE:** 671 G5
KID-FRIENDLY * **WHEELCHAIR/STROLLER ACCESS**

Aerospace Walk of Honor Celebration

LANCASTER CIVIC PLAZA

Lancaster Blvd & Sierra Hwy, Lancaster 93534

661-723-5900 (Special Events Hotline)

www.cityoflancaster.org

Find out what it takes to be a Top Gun flying a F-17 fighter jet at this tribute to aerospace. Pilots, planes and plenty of flying gear from Edwards Air Force Base play a big part in this FREE event that kicks off with a daylong aviation fair. Paint your face in camouflage colors; see real rocket engines and other aviation attractions. Watch the unveiling of a granite monument engraved with the names of five new inductees to the Aerospace Walk of Honor, located at the northeast corner of Lancaster Blvd and Sierra Hwy. Meet some of the honored test pilots and get their autographs. Look for a special afternoon aerial flyby to salute honorees.

WHEN: Sat in Sept
PARKING: FREE * **THOMAS GUIDE:** 4015 H5
KID-FRIENDLY * **WHEELCHAIR/STROLLER ACCESS**

Blessing of the Animals

MARINA GREEN PARK

350 E Shoreline Dr, Long Beach 90802

562-570-3126 (Park)

562-570-3111 (Info)

www.hautedogs.org

Bless your pets with love during this interfaith event held as part of "Animal Appreciation Day" and "Walk for the Animals" hosted by Friends of Long Beach Animals. Clergy from a variety of faiths wave olive branches sprinkled with blessed water and talk or pray for the line-up of pets. All pets—as long as they are well behaved—are welcome to attend this happening sponsored by HauteDogs.org. At least 200 pets and their owners have shown up for previous blessings, which coincide with the Catholic celebration of the Feast of St. Francis (patron saint of animals). You might even meet Spike, the Long Beach Ice Dogs mascot.

WHEN: Noon, last Sun in Sept
PARKING: $7 @ Long Beach Convention Center;
$6 at Aquarium of the Pacific lot
THOMAS GUIDE: 825 E1
KID-FRIENDLY * **WHEELCHAIR/STROLLER ACCESS**

California Coastal Cleanup Day

LA COUNTY AND STATEWIDE BEACHES
1-800-COAST-4U
www.coastal.ca.gov

Show your appreciation for our beautiful beaches and oceans by helping 40,000 volunteers remove trash left by summer crowds. California Coastal Cleanup Day is part of the California Coastal Commission's year-round Adopt-a-Beach program and takes place at shores throughout the state. Over the last two decades this event has resulted in the removal of nearly 8.5 million tons of debris. The cleanup takes place the third Saturday in September from 9AM to Noon. Combined with the Ocean Conservancy's International Coastal Cleanup, which takes place the same day, this three-hour beach sweep is one of the world's largest volunteer events.

WHEN: 3rd Sat morning in Sept
PARKING: Varies * **THOMAS GUIDE:** Varies
KID-FRIENDLY * **WHEELCHAIR/STROLLER ACCESS**

Edwards Air Force Base Open House

EDWARDS AIR FORCE BASE

1 S Rosamond Blvd, Edwards AFB 93524

661-277-3510

www.edwards.af.mil

Marvel at man's ability to soar to new heights during a two-day open house and air show on the western edge of the Mojave Desert, about 90 miles north of downtown LA. Featuring Edwards' top test pilots and flight teams, the event is typically held in the fall. Thrill to the skilled maneuvers of the US Air Force Thunderbirds. Observe aircraft such as the F-16, C-17, B-2 and B-52. Learn about the aircraft systems developed at the Air Force Flight Test Center, NASA Dryden Flight Research Center, the Marine Aircraft Group 46 and others. From the northbound Antelope Valley Freeway (State Hwy 14) take the Rosamond exit; travel east on Rosamond Blvd; follow signs to the West Gate. Travelers can also access the North Gate via Hwy 58.

WHEN: Weekend in Sept or fall
PARKING: FREE * **THOMAS GUIDE:** 3835 H4
KID-FRIENDLY

Family Fishing Derby

HOLLENBECK PARK LAKE

415 S Saint Louis St, LA 90033

1-888-LA-PARKS or 323-261-0113

www.laparks.com

Dip your fishing poles into the last rays of summer at this FREE family fishing competition. Kids and their parents can fish for four hours without a license as part of the State Fish & Game's FREE Fishing Day. Ordinarily, anglers ages 16+ must have a state fishing permit which costs $32.80 annually or $10.50 for a one-day license. Visit learning stations for tips on reeling the fish in. Co-sponsored by the LA City Department of Parks & Recreation, the derby includes a mobile skate park, an appearance by a LA City Fire Department fire truck, community booths and FREE refreshments for fishing participants. Be sure to register—for FREE—in order to be eligible for FREE prizes. Registration starts at 6AM.

WHEN: Sat in Sept, 8AM to Noon, date varies
PARKING: FREE ＊ **THOMAS GUIDE:** 635 A5
KID-FRIENDLY

Harvest Moon Festival

ARCADIA COUNTY PARK
405 S Santa Anita Ave, Arcadia 91007
310-442-2712
www.kscitv.com

Munch on moon cakes while listening to Pan Asian-style hip hop at this annual "Thanksgiving" celebrated by Chinese, Korean and Vietnamese families. Sponsored by KSCI TV, the event attracts 30,000 visitors—many of them with young families—who come to browse the vendor booths, slurp spicy noodles and listen to Asian entertainment. You'll also find the VERB™ at this fest—a moniker for a multi-cultural physical fitness campaign by the Center for Disease Control aimed at tweens, kids ages 9-12. Look for activities that include action verbs—running, jumping and climbing. The 187-acre park has plenty of space for all the activities.

WHEN: Sun in mid-Sept
PARKING: FREE @ Santa Anita Racetrack; FREE shuttle
THOMAS GUIDE: 567 D6
KID-FRIENDLY ＊ WHEELCHAIR/STROLLER ACCESS

LA Greek Fest

SAINT SOPHIA CATHEDRAL
1324 S Normandie Ave, LA 90006
323-737-2424 ext 555
www.lagreekfest.com

Is it all Greek to you? Then dance like Zorba right to the doors of St. Sophia Cathedral in the heart of LA's Byzantine-Latino Quarter. The Zorba Night Greek Dance Contest takes place Friday night during the three-day weekend celebration. Listen to live Greek *bouzouki* as well as Latino music. Hold hands and participate in traditional Greek folk dancing then watch a special Latino show. Let the kids go Greek with arts & crafts. Bring extra *lepta* (money) for the mouth-watering Greek food such as beef & lamb *gyros, loukaniko* (sausage) and *pastistio,* the Greek version of lasagna. Save your sweet tooth for *baklava* and *kourambiethes* (butter cookies dusted with powder sugar). Admission is FREE Friday night. Get in FREE on Sat & Sun by printing out a FREE admission coupon from the Web site. Note: Sometimes held in August.

WHEN: Weekend in Sept or Aug, date varies
PARKING: Pay lots * **THOMAS GUIDE:** 633 J4
KID-FRIENDLY * **WHEELCHAIR/STROLLER ACCESS**

LA Jewish Festival

Location: To Be Determined
818- 464-3230
www.lajewishfestival.org

You'd be *meshuggah* to miss it! This biannual event uses music, exhibits, and games to emphasize *tikkun olam* (social action) themes that can be traced back to the festival's roots as a tool to support Jews in the former Soviet Union. Two stages feature rock, classical, klezmer, and children's music all day. Exhibits from local synagogues and social action groups heighten awareness of the joys of rituals and social involvement. Adventure games for children and adults add to the fun. When it's time for a *nosh*, you'll find dozens of food stands offering a huge variety of kosher meals and snacks. The site of this event varies, so check the Web site for the location of the next festival.

WHEN: To Be Determined
PARKING: Varies ★ **THOMAS GUIDE:** Varies
KID-FRIENDLY ★ **WHEELCHAIR/STROLLER ACCESS**

LA Korean Festival

SEOUL INTERNATIONAL PARK, KOREATOWN
3250 San Marino St, LA 90006
213-487-9696
www.lakoreanfestival.com

Discover the soul of the Korean people in Seoul Park during this four-day festival that has embraced Koreatown and the surrounding communities for 30+ years. Let the aroma of barbecue pork and kimchee guide you to the heart of the FREE festival inside the park where the main performing stage, business expo and international food court are located. Watch and listen to FREE Korean and World Culture performances including music, dance and drama. Visit 160+ booths where businesses promote and sell their services and products. A carnival adjacent to the park charges fees for games and rides. Don't miss the colorful parade that marches down Olympic Blvd between Vermont & Western Aves on Saturday afternoon.

WHEN: Thu – Sun in Sept, dates vary; parade on Sat afternoon
PARKING: FREE in nearby structure, FREE shuttle**THOMAS GUIDE:** 633 J3
KID-FRIENDLY ★ **WHEELCHAIR/STROLLER ACCESS**

LA Latino Book & Family Festival

EAST LOS ANGELES COLLEGE

1301 Avenida Cesar Chavez, Monterey Park 91754

760-434-4484

www.latinobookfestival.com

Say *bienvenidos* to books, learning, and health in your family's life. A love of Latino and Latina literature can start or be encouraged with a visit to this two-day festival, which aims to advance the cause of literacy and love of reading in the Hispanic community. The fair is comprised of seven themed villages: Books, Careers, Education & Technology, Children's, Culture & Travel, Health, and Mi Casita. Each area contains programs and activities which target the improvement of living standards for Latinos including book readings and signings, seminars on resume preparation, information on higher education, lectures on the importance of health screenings, and exhibits on home ownership. Also, child and adult writing and art exhibitions are held. A kid's play area is available. Two food courts allow visitors to refuel and refresh themselves with *antojitos* (Mexican appetizers) and *refrescos* (cold drinks).

WHEN: Sat – Sun in Sept
PARKING: Limited at FREE lot, street parking
THOMAS GUIDE: 635 H/J5
KID-FRIENDLY * WHEELCHAIR/STROLLER ACCESS

LA Moon Festival

CENTRAL PLAZA, CHINATOWN

900 to 1000 N Broadway, LA 90012

213-680-0243

www.lamoonfestival.com

Welcome autumn and celebrate the bounty of the summer harvest at this traditional Chinese festival held around the

15th day of the 8th lunar month. Dating back over a 1,000 years in China, this fest has been gaining popularity in LA with about 5,000 visitors attending the local celebration. Discover how to bring the art of *feng shui* into your life at the event, which happens near Chung King Road, an area that's becoming a vibrant art colony. FREE entertainment includes Chinese acrobatics, Asian-American bands and martial arts demonstrations. Be sure to buy a traditional moon cake from one of the Asian food vendors—the special sweet cake fillings include red bean and lotus seed pastes. Zoom in on the full moon through telescopes provided near the main stage at the fest's end.

WHEN: Sat in mid-Sept
PARKING: Pay lots, metered street ∗ **THOMAS GUIDE:** 634 G2
KID-FRIENDLY ∗ **WHEELCHAIR/STROLLER ACCESS**

LA's Birthday Bash

EL PUEBLO DE LOS ANGELES HISTORIC MONUMENT
125 Paseo de la Plaza (Olvera Street), LA 90012
213-625-5045
www.olvera-street.com

Commemorate the founding of our metropolis with artisan demos, historic re-enactments, and, of course, food and entertainment. Olvera Street, the oldest part of LA, resurrected in 1930 and converted into a Mexican market place by Christine Sterling, is now officially part of El Pueblo de Los Angeles Historical Monument. Here on Sept 4, 1781, settlers from the San Gabriel Mission stopped after a nine-mile trek and established what became the City of Angels. (See Los Pobladores event this chapter) FREE entertainment includes dramatic presentations, folklorico and mariachis. There are historic tours, shops, and restaurants. Stick around for the FREE *piñata* and birthday cake!

WHEN: Sept 4
PARKING: Pay lots, metered street ∗ **THOMAS GUIDE:** 634 G3
KID-FRIENDLY ∗ **HISTORIC** ∗ **WHEELCHAIR/STROLLER ACCESS**

La Fiesta de San Gabriel

SAN GABRIEL MISSION
428 S Mission Dr, San Gabriel 91776
626-457-3035
www.sangabrielmission.org

Visit the "Pride of the California Missions" for a weekend celebration and commemoration of the birthplace of the Los Angeles region. Including international foods, games and rides, this festival celebrates the area's historic diversity. Founded by Father Junipero Serra and the Tongva Indians on September 8, 1771, it was from this mission that the original *Pobladores,* a group of Spanish, Africans, and Mestizos, set off to found LA. The festival's opening ceremonies include the reenactment of this walk, which culminates in LA's Birthday Bash at Olvera Street. Not up for a nine-mile hike? Stay then, for mass, the blessing of the animals, door prizes, and live entertainment. Note: Sometimes held in late August.

WHEN: Weekend in late Aug or early Sept
PARKING: FREE * **THOMAS GUIDE:** 596 D4
KID-FRIENDLY * **HISTORIC** * **WHEELCHAIR/STROLLER ACCESS**

Latin American Heritage Celebration

ANGELUS PLAZA
255 S Hill St at 2nd St, LA 90012
213-623-4352 ext 327
www.ci.la.ca.us

Delight in Latin American music and dance in all its amazing variety. Held on the courtyard of downtown's Angelus Plaza, the two-hour program brings together performers from North, Central, and South America as well as the Caribbean Islands. Visitors can listen to salsa, Afro-Cuban, bossa nova, folk, and mariachi music while watching colorful dance shows inspired by rich Latin traditions and cultures from Chicago to Santiago. The celebration, produced by the LA Cultural Affairs Office, is designed to promote harmony and an appreciation of cultural diversity among the multi-ethnic population of the mid-city area.

WHEN: Fri afternoon in mid-Sept
PARKING: Pay lots and structures, fees vary ∗ **THOMAS GUIDE:** 634 F3
KID-FRIENDLY ∗ **WHEELCHAIR/STROLLER ACCESS**

Latinos in Hollywood Exhibit

Location: To Be Determined
310-274-6234
www.olvera-street.com/latinos_in_hollywood.html

View a panorama of Latino luminaries of the silver screen. With over 160+ photographs, this exhibition brings to life the history and achievements of motion picture and television actors, producers, directors, writers, and behind-the-scenes workers of Latin heritage. Snapshots of stars such as Dolores Del Rio, Rita Moreno, Margarita Cansino (better known as Rita Hayworth), Andy Garcia, Jimmy Smits, and many others are displayed. The exhibition is presented as part of Latino Heritage Month. The site of this exhibition varies so check the Web site for the location of its next showing.

WHEN: To Be Determined
PARKING: Varies ∗ **THOMAS GUIDE:** Varies

Los Pobladores

SAN GABRIEL MISSION
428 S Mission Dr, San Gabriel 91776
626-457-3035
www.sangabrielmission.org

Re-live history when you join the descendants of the first settlers of Los Angeles and retrace the original trail from the San Gabriel Mission to Olvera Street. Over two hundred years ago, eleven families set off to found the Pueblo of Los Angeles where Governor de Neve had promised them new homes. Traveling through Arizona, Baja and Alta California, they paused at the San Gabriel mission where they rested up, geared up, and started off again. They settled along what we now call the LA River. One of the sponsors of this nine-mile trek is Los Pobladores 200, the descendants of the founding families. Anticipate a three-hour walk, a rest stop at Lincoln Park, and comfort vans cruising the route. Fee for return transportation.

WHEN: Labor Day, first Mon in Sept
PARKING: FREE in the mission parking lot * **THOMAS GUIDE:** 596 D4
HISTORIC

Manhattan Beach Arts Festival

MANHATTAN BEACH BOULEVARD

Between Valley Dr & Highland Ave, Manhattan Beach 90266
310-802-5440
www.ci.manhattan-beach.ca.us

You'll take Manhattan—Beach that is—when you visit this South Bay fair that emphasizes art education for adults and kids. Visit the dance stage and learn steps from the South Pacific, British Isles, South America and other far-off lands. Check out the music stage and listen to swing, Dixieland, and drum jams. Bring the kids to the children's stage to see performances by students from nearby schools and then to Kreativity Korner where they can join in art and music-making workshops. Laugh at the outrageously fun street entertainers. A food court features booths with goodies from local eateries.

WHEN: 2nd Sun in Sept
PARKING: FREE limited street parking, pay parking lots
THOMAS GUIDE: 732 F6
KID-FRIENDLY * **WHEELCHAIR/STROLLER ACCESS**

Mexican Independence Day

EL PUEBLO DE LOS ANGELES HISTORIC MONUMENT
125 Paseo de la Plaza (Olvera Street), LA 90012
213-625-5045
www.olvera-street.com

Viva Mexico! Mexican-Americans shout it proud in tribute to Miguel Hidalgo y Costilla, an old activist priest in Dolores, Mexico whose *grito* (shout) of those words near Midnight on Sept. 15, 1810, called for locals to fight Spain's 300-year occupation of Mexico. The dates of Sept 15–16 have come to be recognized in the US as Mexican Independence Day, when Mexican-Americans celebrate their heritage. On a weekend close to these dates, green, white and red decorations (the colors of Mexico's flag) stand out on Olvera Street, the Mexican marketplace located in LA's historic birthplace. The street and plaza are filled with FREE activities, historic displays, artisan exhibits and vibrant dance and music performances.

WHEN: Around Sept 15
PARKING: Metered street, pay public lots * **THOMAS GUIDE:** 634 G3
KID-FRIENDLY * **HISTORIC** * **WHEELCHAIR/STROLLER ACCESS**

Thai Cultural Day

BARNSDALL ART PARK
4800 Hollywood Blvd, Hollywood 90027
213-485-5481 (Art Park)
310-827-2910 (Thai Community Arts & Cultural Center)
www.thaiculturalcenter.org

Thai yourself up in Asian culture at this one-day FREE festival that brings Thailand's music, art, sports, design and of course, food, to this popular park. Look for the elaborate costumes and ornate headdresses worn by performers in dance presentations, the Thai costume contest and the cultural parade that starts before Noon on Hollywood Blvd between Western and Vermont Avenues. Be sure to catch one of the storytelling dance performances where each movement has a special meaning. Watch the FREE Thai food demonstrations and intricate vegetable carving then satisfy your hunger at the food vendors selling pad Thai noodles, garlic shrimp and panang curry.

WHEN: Sat in Sept, date varies
PARKING: FREE * **THOMAS GUIDE:** 593 G4
KID-FRIENDLY * **WHEELCHAIR/STROLLER ACCESS**

UCLA Extension Writers Faire

YOUNG HALL COURTYARD, UCLA

405 Hilgard Ave, LA 90095

310-825-9415

www.uclaextension.edu

Got the write stuff? Then find out how to take your skills to the next level. Held the second Saturday in September, this festival has 60+ professional writers and writing instructors available to help advise you about honing your craft and selling your work. 24 mini-classes and panels teach pertinent topics in creative writing and screenwriting. Meet with representatives from local writers organizations to learn how joining with other writers can open networking opportunities and provide valuable knowledge of the art and business of writing. Discuss educational opportunities with counselors from local colleges that offer advanced degrees in creative writing. Receive a 10% discount on fall Writers Program courses at UCLA. FREE refreshments provided.

WHEN: 2nd Sat in Sept
PARKING: On campus $7 * **THOMAS GUIDE:** 632 B1 & 2
WHEELCHAIR ACCESS

Watts Towers Day of the Drum Festival

THE WATTS TOWERS ARTS CENTER
1727 E 107th St, LA 90002
213-847-4646
www.trywatts.com

Listen to the beat of your own drummer at this FREE community festival that spins into a jazz fest the following day. Discover, celebrate and tap the drums that have played a role in world cultures from Aztec to African. What better place to drum up creativity than at these towers created by Simon Rodia, an Italian immigrant tile setter who followed his own rhythm and determinedly built 17 mosaic towers piece by piece. The towers are one of only nine works of folk art listed on the National Register of Historic Places. Kids create their own works of art in the children's area and all visitors should see the arts center's percussion instrument exhibit donated by renowned collector Dr. Joseph Howard. Participate in the Citywide Universal Drum Circle both days, too.

WHEN: Last Sat in Sept
PARKING: Pay lots, metered street * **THOMAS GUIDE:** 704 G5
KID-FRIENDLY * **WHEELCHAIR/STROLLER ACCESS**

Watts Towers Jazz Festival

1727 E 107th St, LA 90002
213-847-4646
www.trywatts.com

Follow up the Day of the Drum festival with eight hours of heart-pounding performances from Latin rhythms to gospel to jazz with a classical twist. Top jazz percussionists and pianists head the line-up at one of LA's longest running jazz events. Traditional jazz is interspersed with African dance troupes, hip-hop poets and avant-garde artists. Plenty of FREE kids' art activities and multi-media exhibits in the arts center including screenings of the previous year's drum & jazz fests.

WHEN: Last Sun in Sept
PARKING: Pay lots, metered street * **THOMAS GUIDE:** 704 G5
KID-FRIENDLY * **WHEELCHAIR/STROLLER ACCESS**

Art's Alive Festival

TORRANCE CULTURAL ARTS CENTER

3330 Civic Center Dr, Torrance 90036

310-781-7150

www.tcac.torrnet.com

Express yourself creatively through visual, performing and literary arts at this two-day event that's alive with hands-on activities featuring music, dance, theatre, crafts and fine arts. Enjoy clay sculpting, jewelry making and origami folding. FREE face painting and balloon animals for kids. The South Bay Quilters Guild, the Handweavers Guild and the Freeway Lace Guild demonstrate their techniques and provide displays on the history of their crafts. FREE dance and musical entertainment on two stages plus vendor booths, an art exhibit and a juried art show.

WHEN: Sat — Sun in Oct, dates vary
PARKING: FREE
THOMAS GUIDE: 763 E5
KID-FRIENDLY ✷ WHEELCHAIR/STROLLER ACCESS

Arts Open House

LANCASTER PERFORMING ARTS CENTER
750 Lancaster Blvd, Lancaster 93535
661-723-5950
www.lpac.org

Indulge in a cultural potpourri organized by the Lancaster Performing Arts Center Foundation. The celebration features work from talented local artists and area high school students as well as poetry readings by Antelope Valley amateur and professional writers. Musicians from classical to western to hip-hop and rock provide entertainment. Glean a world of information from the numerous local arts organizations that set up question-and-answer booths. Usually held the first Saturday in October, the event strives to provide arts and culture to all—from toddlers to senior citizens.

WHEN: 1st Sat in Oct
PARKING: FREE * **THOMAS GUIDE:** 4016 A6
KID-FRIENDLY * **WHEELCHAIR/STROLLER ACCESS**

Autumn Sea Festival

CABRILLO MARINE AQUARIUM
3720 Stephen White Dr, San Pedro 90731
310-548-7562
www.cabrilloaq.org

Search for real buried treasure and other fun-in-the-sun activities at this seaworthy celebration. True pirates from the Brethren of the Coast band hand out treasure maps with clues to two pirate chests buried on Cabrillo Beach. Find them and the treasure is yours. Not up for cutthroat competition? Then enter the daylong sand sculpture contest or observe a top sand sculpture artist create a masterpiece with two tons of sand. Watch Queen of the Sea contestants parade in unique marine-themed costumes or enter the pageant yourself—the contest is open to all genders. Play hometown-style fair games (25-cents each) designed by aquarium staffers or enjoy the FREE face-painting, puppet shows and live entertainment.

WHEN: 3rd Sun in Oct
PARKING: FREE, 22nd and Miner Streets;
FREE shuttle; $7 per car at Cabrillo Beach
THOMAS GUIDE: 854 C2
KID-FRIENDLY

Bicycle Rodeo

YERBA BUENA ELEMENTARY SCHOOL
5844 Larboard Ln, Agoura Hills 91301
818-597-7361
www.ci.agoura-hills.ca.us

Get in gear when kids learn and practice bicycle skills at the City of Agoura Hills's bicycle rodeo. Sponsored by the LA County Sheriff's Department and Auto Club of Southern California, the rodeo site features stations where young bicyclists receive instruction on balancing, braking, mounting, and signaling. Bikers get help with seat adjustment, helmet fitting and tire inflation. A FREE professional BMX stunt show rounds out a day of biking bliss.

WHEN: Sat in Oct, date varies
PARKING: FREE ∗ **THOMAS GUIDE:** 557 G4
KID-FRIENDLY ∗ **WHEELCHAIR/STROLLER ACCESS**

Calabasas Cultural Festival

OLDTOWN CALABASAS
23537 Calabasas Rd, Calabasas 91302
818-878-4225 ext. 270
www.cityofcalabasas.com

Steep yourself in the West San Fernando Valley's colorful, yet little-known cultural history while browsing the wares of today's artisans, listening to live music and enjoying dance performances at the three-acre historic Leonis Adobe site in Old Town Calabasas. Originally built in 1844, the adobe was enlarged and extensively remodeled in 1880 by its most famous owner, Miguel Leonis, a Basque immigrant whose power and fame earned him the symbolic moniker "The King of Calabasas." Festival visitors get FREE admission to the adobe and neighboring Plummer House, participate in FREE art classes, view wildlife exhibits, and watch demonstrations of butter churning, yarn spinning, lassoing, and livestock feeding. For a break from the activities, stroll a few feet east of the adobe to the tiny but lush Calabasas Creek Park.

WHEN: 1st Sat – Sun in Oct
PARKING: FREE lot, street * **THOMAS GUIDE:** 559 F4
KID-FRIENDLY * **HISTORIC** * **WHEELCHAIR/STROLLER ACCESS**

California Wildlife Center Open House

CALIFORNIA WILDLIFE CENTER
26026 Piuma Rd, Calabasas 91302
310-458-WILD
www.californiawildlifecenter.org

Learn how the California Wildlife Center rescues sick and injured wild animals during one of the center's semi-annual open houses. One open house is held the third week in April to coincide with National Wildlife Week; the other is held in October. The volunteer staff uses lectures, photographs, and a video to show how the animals are healed, rehabilitated and released back into the wild. The center also has exhibits that display information about the history of area wildlife. Located in the Santa Monica Mountains near the Calabasas-Malibu border, the center is housed in an old ranger station that was converted to an animal hospital in 1998. On State Park property, the center operates with the permission of the California State Park Service.

Because of the animals' fragile physical and emotional condition, they cannot be shown to the public at these events. Visitors must call 310-458-WILD to RSVP and to obtain directions and further information.

WHEN: 3rd week in Apr, weekend in Oct
PARKING: FREE * **THOMAS GUIDE:** 628 H1
KID-FRIENDLY

Chalk on the Walk

PALMDALE PLAYHOUSE
38334 10th St East, Palmdale 93550
661-267-5685
www.cityofpalmdale.org

Paint the town or at least the pavement, in a brilliant rainbow of chalk colors during this popular event, a highlight of the Palmdale Playhouse's three-day Children's Festival. Kids exhibit their artistic abilities by drawing scenes of their choice—a mountain with an eagle soaring overhead, a pond with ducks floating, or perhaps a likeness of their best friend—on sidewalks near the playhouse during a one-hour period of FREE expression. After releasing their creative energy, youngsters can satisfy their hunger by munching on hot dogs, chips and soda available for purchase. Usually held the first or second weekend in October.

WHEN: 1st or 2nd weekend in Oct
PARKING: FREE in public lot * **THOMAS GUIDE:** 4286 B1
KID-FRIENDLY * **WHEELCHAIR/STROLLER ACCESS**

Children's Cultural Festival

LONG BEACH MUSEUM OF ART
2300 E Ocean Blvd, Long Beach 90803
www.lbma.org

Paint yourself silly at one of most popular events at the Long Beach Museum of Art. Drawing more than 2,000 kids and their families, the FREE festival has been providing a rainbow of art-making activities for 17+ years. Experience creative global traditions with FREE workshops, live performances and storytelling. Create Venetian carnival masks, Chinese paper lanterns, Korean paper fans, Chilean rain sticks and Native American necklaces. Explore the museum's exhibits, including its collection of 300 years of American decorative arts objects, for FREE. And it's all on a bluff overlooking the shimmering Pacific Ocean.

WHEN: Last Sat afternoon in Oct
PARKING: FREE * **THOMAS GUIDE:** 825 G1
KID-FRIENDLY * **WHEELCHAIR/STROLLER ACCESS**

Día de los Muertos en Hollywood

HOLLYWOOD FOREVER CEMETERY

6000 Santa Monica Blvd, Hollywood 90038
323-469-1181
www.ladayofthedead.com

Only in LA can you find the only cemetery in California that celebrates this traditional and sacred Hispanic holiday, which bridges the gap between the living and the dead. Based on ancient Aztec ceremonies, the day is a way for the living to mock death and to honor dead relatives at the same time. Unlike the scare-your-pants-off quality of Halloween, the Day of the Dead comes alive with cultural rituals. Walking among the dead (including Hollywood celebrities) on torch-lit paths, visitors are greeted by Aztec music, 20-foot-tall walking skeletons and ornate altars. A highlight of the event, the altars are exquisite folk art pieces whose creators have spent weeks constructing them in tribute to their deceased loved ones. The festivities at the cemetery include costumed ceremonial dancers, theatre presentations, art and photo exhibits.

WHEN: Last Sat in Oct
PARKING: FREE ★ **THOMAS GUIDE:** 593 G5
KID-FRIENDLY ★ **HISTORIC** ★ **WHEELCHAIR/STROLLER ACCESS**

Eagle Rock Community Cultural Association's Music Festival

CENTER FOR THE ARTS, EAGLE ROCK
2225 Colorado Blvd, Eagle Rock 90041
323-226-1617
www.erccc.org

Tango your soul out, be mesmerized by Japanese drummers or schmooze with LA politicos at the opening night ceremonies. From Copland to hip-hop, from Latin rock to zydeco, this two-day FREE music fest is a crowd pleaser. Featuring hip acts like Quetzal, as well as reggae bands, blues artists, world music and more, previous festivals have hosted FREE entertainment at 20+ eclectic venues along Colorado Boulevard, including coffee houses, restaurants and gas stations, all linked by FREE shuttles. Come, hear the music play!

WHEN: Sat – Sun in Oct, dates vary
PARKING: Varies; FREE shuttles ★ **THOMAS GUIDE:** 564 H5
KID-FRIENDLY

Fall Festival

LA FARMER'S MARKET
6333 W Third St, LA 90036
323-933-9211
www.farmersmarketla.com

Harvest a bumper crop of country-style fall fun without leaving the city. Historic LA Farmers Market holds its weekend-long tribute to the season in late October with activities that include hayrides, pumpkin carving, square danc-ing and gardening displays. Kids enjoy the petting zoo and craft demonstrations. Live music serenades visitors all weekend.

WHEN: Weekend in late Oct
PARKING: FREE lot * **THOMAS GUIDE:** 633 B1
KID-FRIENDLY * HISTORIC * WHEELCHAIR/STROLLER ACCESSIBLE

International Festival of Masks

HANCOCK PARK
5814 Wilshire Blvd, LA 90036
323-937-4230
www.cafam.org

Put on a new face at this celebration of masks from around the world that's been a local favorite for 25+ years. Hosted by the Craft & Folk Art Museum, the fun fest is held across the street at Hancock Park, home to the LA County Museum of Art, the George C. Page Museum and the La Brea Tar Pits. Learn about traditional mask-making then participate in creating your own with FREE hands-on art activities sponsored by several museums and cultural institutions. Masks of all kinds—beaded, woven, molded, feathered, sequined—are for sale, and a line-up of FREE entertain-ment features ethnic music, dance and storytelling. Look for the Parade of Masks, a colorful procession filled with masked characters ranging from Chinese dragons to American Indian eagle dancers. See a wonderful depiction of this scene in a 60-foot-long mural at the Wilshire-Normandie Metro Rail Station, painted by renowned mural-ist Frank Romero.

WHEN: Sat in Oct, date varies
PARKING: Metered street, pay lots * **THOMAS GUIDE:** 633 C2
KID-FRIENDLY * WHEELCHAIR/STROLLER ACCESS

LA Times Festival of Health and Fitness

UNIVERSITY OF SOUTHERN CALIFORNIA
University Park Campus, LA 90089
213-740-6786
www.latimesevents.com

Learn how to get well. Learn how to stay well. Learn to have fun doing both. This weekend-long fair is a colossus of information on healing with nearly 50 panels and workshops including fitness demonstrations and yoga instruction. Hear lectures on choosing a health plan, improving nutrition, acquiring good fitness habits, and evaluating alternative therapies. Listen to celebrities and LA Times columnists and writers discuss cutting-edge concepts in nutrition, weight loss and chronic disease control. Get health screenings including FREE blood pressure, diabetes and blood panel testing as well as low-cost immunizations for children and prostate cancer and thyroid checks. Watch healthy-cooking demonstrations by well-known chefs and cookbook authors. Volleyball, soccer, and other sports clinics show you how fitness and fun are a great fit. Live swing, salsa, alt-rock, and jazz fill the air, while flamenco and ballet dancers glide on stage.

WHEN: Sat – Sun in Oct, dates vary
PARKING: On campus $5 * **THOMAS GUIDE:** 674 B1
KID-FRIENDLY * **WHEELCHAIR/STROLLER ACCESS**

Latino History Parade & Festival

WASHINGTON PARK
700 E Washington Blvd, Pasadena 91104
626-791-7421
www.latinohistoryparade.org

Viva! Latino history at this parade and festival sponsored by the Latino Heritage Association that not only honors

Latinos but the cultural diversity of the Pasadena area as well. Starting at Los Robles Street north of Washington Blvd, the parade includes marchers in bright folkloric costumes and students and staff from the Pasadena Unified School District. Discover a broad range of Latino traditions and customs at the post-parade *Jamaica* (festival) at Washington Park. Tapping into the colorful history of Californio, the celebration has included a re-enactment of an elaborate wedding from the 1840s. Participate in historic games, crafts and skills such as such as playing the Mayan *bubalak* (water drum made from a gourd). The FREE fun includes festive music and dance.

WHEN: Sat in Oct, date varies; Noon to 1PM for parade
PARKING: FREE * **THOMAS GUIDE:** 566 A1
KID-FRIENDLY * **HISTORIC** * **WHEELCHAIR/STROLLER ACCESS**

Long Beach International City Bank Marathon

STARTING LINE: SHORELINE DR
West of Linden Ave, Long Beach 90802
562-728-8829
www.runlongbeach.com

Run to the beach and qualify for any marathon in the country including the Boston Marathon, when you compete in this 26.2-mile course. The marathon not only meets certification standards, but also outshines other races for its beachside location. Sponsored by International City Bank, runners from around the globe return every year to race past the majestic Queen Mary ocean liner, through miles of shoreline bike paths, past a lagoon, a historic rancho, and verdant parks. Spectators can cheer on the thousands of runners at this surfside location for FREE. It costs $80 to officially enter the race unless you prefer to try the half-marathon, inline skate marathon, bike tour or 5K run. Stick around for the FREE post-race Finish Line Festival. Finish

Line is adjacent to Marina Green Park. (See separate event this chapter)

WHEN: 2nd Sun of Oct
PARKING: $8 at the Long Beach Convention Center lot behind the Long Beach Arena
THOMAS GUIDE: 825 D1

Long Beach International City Bank Marathon Expo

LONG BEACH CONVENTION CENTER

300 E Ocean Blvd, Long Beach 90802
562-436-3636 (Convention Center)
562-728-8829 (Marathon Office)
www.runlongbeach.com

Load up on the latest sports health info and learn about all the new high-tech fitness equipment at this FREE expo bursting with vendor booths. Discover what it takes to maintain an active and healthy lifestyle. FREE for anyone who's interested in racking up their fitness up a notch, the expo is also the mandatory pick-up location for all marathon runners' registration materials. It's here that marathoners get their FREE T-shirt and goodie bag packed with FREEbies including a FREE admission ticket to the Aquarium of the Pacific.

WHEN: Fri – Sat before marathon
PARKING: $8 convention center parking lot * **THOMAS GUIDE:** 825 E1
KID-FRIENDLY * **WHEELCHAIR/STROLLER ACCESS**

Long Beach International City Bank Marathon Finish Line Festival

MARINA GREEN PARK
350 E Shoreline Dr, Long Beach 90802
562-570-3126 (Park)
562-728-8829 (Marathon Office)
www.runlongbeach.com

Jog over to Marina Green Park and keep an eye on the finish line, just steps away from the beach. Keep track of the action as the runners hit the last downhill yards on Shoreline Drive or watch the sailboats glide by as you wait for the athletes to cross the finish line. Afterward, help your racing friends and family recuperate from their hours of pounding the pavement. Chill out on The Green picnic, style or hang out at the beer garden and listen to the beat of the FREE pop concert.

WHEN: Marathon Day, 2nd Sun of Oct
PARKING: $8 convention center parking lot * **THOMAS GUIDE:** 825 E1
KID-FRIENDLY * **WHEELCHAIR/STROLLER ACCESS**

NoHo Children's Art & Poetry Festival

THEATRE OF HOPE, INC & YOUTH SPIRIT
5220 Lankershim Blvd, North Hollywood 91601
818-779-2101
www.thaw.org

Share the love of visual and theatre arts with children at this daylong fest that offers 20+ FREE workshops. Hundreds of volunteers help with this multi-cultural arts enrichment experience for families. Located in front of the Academy of Television Arts & Sciences, the center provides all the materials to create rain sticks, hand puppets, wind chimes, masks, *piñatas*, peace flags and jewelry. Get funky at the hip-hop poetry jam, learn how to tango and make your family laugh with improvisational skits. Take time out from the art groove to enjoy the FREE family entertainment on the main stage.

WHEN: Sat in Oct
PARKING: Metered street, pay lots * **THOMAS GUIDE:** 562 J2
KID-FRIENDLY * **WHEELCHAIR/STROLLER ACCESS**

Old West Fest

MUSEUM OF THE AMERICAN WEST
4700 Western Heritage Way, LA 90027
323-667-2000
www.autry-museum.org

Giddyap! to the museum for the annual western heritage fest and rope yourself a herd of cowboy culture, music and poetry. Meet on the South Lawn for FREE western-style entertainment. Give your lungs a workout at the family yodeling workshops, watch re-enactment groups present skits and demonstrations. Past performers have included Devon Dawson, the voice of "Jessy the Yodelin' Cowgirl" from Toy Story II and Sourdough Slim, a yodelin' accordion player. The Wells Fargo Theatre features 30+ Western acts —each show is $10 for museum members, $15 for non-members. Full festival pass is $45 for members, $65 for non-members. Remember, pardner, South Lawn activities are FREE; museum admission and theatre shows require full saddlebags.

WHEN: Sat in Oct, date varies
PARKING: FREE * **THOMAS GUIDE:** 564 B5
KID-FRIENDLY * **WHEELCHAIR/STROLLER ACCESS**

Pasadena Art Night

ART CENTER COLLEGE OF DESIGN

1700 Lida St, Pasadena 91103

626-396-2200

www.artcenter.edu/artnight

Frugal culture vultures swoop into Pasadena two nights a year (Oct & Mar) to take advantage of FREE admission to 12 cultural venues, including 6 major museums. Dazzling Impressionists shimmer at the Norton Simon Museum, ancient Buddhist artifacts shine at the Pacific Asia Museum. Hop on the FREE shuttle stopping at each venue and admire contemporary exhibits at the Armory Center for the Arts, Armory Northwest, Pasadena Museum of California Art, and a more historical perspective from the Pasadena Museum of California Art and Pasadena Museum of History. Attend the Pasadena Symphony Orchestra's open rehearsal. Become part of the orchestra at the Pasadena Conservatory of Music's Music Mobile®. Listen to music under the stars as the Pasadena Pops Orchestra serenades visitors at the Levitt Pavilion. View cutting edge art at the Art Center College of Design's Williamson Gallery and new installations at Pasadena City College's George Boone Sculpture Garden.

WHEN: 6PM to 10PM, Fri in Oct & Mar, dates vary
PARKING: FREE at Art Center College of Design
or Norton Simon Museum; FREE shuttle
THOMAS GUIDE: 565 D1
KID-FRIENDLY

Pioneer Days

MEMORIAL PARK

222 W Sierra Madre Blvd, Sierra Madre 91024

626-355-5111

www.sierramadrepioneerdays.com

Sierra Madre, that quiet hamlet in the San Gabriel foothills, perks up around the first and second weekends in October when the city honors and celebrates its past. Old-timers and history buffs gather in Memorial Park with historical tales, slide shows, and memorabilia. Of particular interest are items and photos pertaining to the dozens of camps that dotted the San Gabriel Mountains during the early 20th century. Kids can take part in panning for gold, bobbing for apples and having a go at washing clothes -- pioneer style. Historic buildings are open to the public including Lizzie's Trail Inn, a one-time supply station for pack trains and hikers climbing the Old Mt. Wilson Trail (and a former restaurant) that's been restored and converted to a museum. The Ward Ranch, the only farm left in town, offers crafts exhibits, live entertainment and a classic car display.

WHEN: Weekend in Oct, dates vary
PARKING: FREE on city streets * **THOMAS GUIDE:** 567 A2
KID-FRIENDLY * HISTORIC * WHEELCHAIR/STROLLER ACCESS

Teacher Day at the Garden

RANCHO SANTA ANA BOTANIC GARDEN

1500 N College Ave, Claremont 91711

909-625-8767, ext. 224

www.rsabg.org

Go out to the garden—the Rancho Santa Ana Botanical Garden—and discover how a garden field trip can enhance the classroom teaching experience. FREE for teachers and administrators, this day in the garden shows educators how they can cultivate new teaching concepts by using garden field trips to enrich their curriculum in language arts, science, social studies and art. Sprout new teaching methods by exchanging ideas with other educators, unearthing FREE teaching resources and digging into the garden's outreach loan kits, tours and school programs. FREE light refreshments.

WHEN: Sat in Oct, date varies
PARKING: FREE * **THOMAS GUIDE:** 601 F1

Teacher Open House @ Aquarium of the Pacific

AQUARIUM OF THE PACIFIC
100 Aquarium Way, Long Beach 90802
562-951-1630 or 888-826-7257
www.aquariumofpacific.org

Surf with the sharks and wing it with the lorikeets for FREE at this open house for educators only, sponsored by the Boeing Company. Tour the aquarium galleries swimming with brilliant sea life. Feed the colorful birds in the Lorikeet Forest. Meet the education staff, observe classroom demonstrations and watch theater presentations. Learn about the aquarium's educational resources including the "Aquarium on Wheels" and take 20 percent off membership and all gift store purchases. Bring one guest for FREE and enter to win a FREE 25-gallon classroom aquarium or a FREE sponsorship for the "Adopt an Animal" program. FREE light refreshments. Reservations are required.

WHEN: Weeknight in Oct
PARKING: FREE * **THOMAS GUIDE:** 825 D1
WHEELCHAIR ACCESS

West Hollywood Book Fair

WEST HOLLYWOOD PARK

647 N San Vicente Blvd, West Hollywood 90069

323-848-6431

www.weho.org

Book yourself for a day of literary locomotion in a town that prides itself on its bevy of bookstores and its residents' love of literature. The West Hollywood Book Fair takes place in early autumn and is dedicated to the encouragement of reading, writing, and literacy. Nearly 200 authors, actors and spoken word artists appear, many of who participate in discussions about their work and literature in general. Recent participants have included Carol Channing, Lalo Alcarez, Trey Ellis, Gil Garcetti, Arianna Huffington, Kelly Lange, Marlee Matlin and Christopher Rice. Attend poetry slams, author salons and writing workshops. Visit 40+ booths hosted by bookstores, publishers, and literary non-profit organizations. Note: Sometimes held in September.

WHEN: Sun in Oct or Sept
PARKING: Pay lots, limited FREE street parking
THOMAS GUIDE: 592 H7
WHEELCHAIR/STROLLER ACCESS

Note
FIND FREE
HALLOWEEN
EVENTS UNDER
HOLIDAYS
*

NOVEMBER

College and Career Convention

LA CONVENTION CENTER
1201 S Figueroa St, LA 90015
213-482-9847
www.lafreecashforcollege.org

Grab your piece of the multi-million dollar financial-aid pie and get a running start on your educational and career paths. For soon-to-be high school grads and workers who want to return to school, this convention has morning and evening sessions packed with college & career information. Speak with financial aid counselors and attend scholarship sessions throughout the day. Visit 100+ exhibitors showcasing public and private universities, community colleges, and trade and technical schools. Attend workshops on choosing a college, selecting a major and finding educational resources for recent immigrants.

WHEN: mid-Nov
PARKING: Pay structure, $10; pay lots, fees vary * **THOMAS GUIDE:** 634 D5
WHEELCHAIR ACCESS

Dia de Los Muertos en Olvera Street

EL PUEBLO DE LOS ANGELES HISTORIC MONUMENT
125 Paseo de la Plaza (Olvera Street), LA 90012
213-625-5045
www.olvera-street.com

Pay homage to deceased loved ones and discover the heritage of the Hispanic Day of the Dead celebration. With its roots in Aztec culture, Dia de los Muertos gives celebrants a chance to face death joyously while also remembering dead ancestors. Elaborate altars are carried during processions held on the Christian holidays of All Saints Day (Nov 1) and All Souls Day (Nov 2). During the week before, Olvera Street features altar displays and daily *piñata* breaking. In the mornings there are FREE children's art workshops for ancestor-honoring projects including mask coloring, necklace making and flower painting. On Nov 1 & 2, Olvera Street is filled with colorful processions, ballet folklorico and authentic Aztec ceremonial dancing. Look for special *pan de muertos* (bread of the dead) on Nov. 2. Learn more about the rituals by watching the FREE Day of the Dead video at the Olvera Street Visitor Center located in the historic Sepulveda House.

WHEN: Nov 1 to 2 and the week prior
PARKING: Pay lots, metered street ∗ **THOMAS GUIDE:** 634 G3
KID-FRIENDLY ∗ **HISTORIC** ∗ **WHEELCHAIR/STROLLER ACCESS**

Long Beach Veterans Day Parade

HOUGHTON PARK
Atlantic Ave & E Harding St, Long Beach 90805
562-570-6137
www.veteransdayparade.com

Salute the men and women who have served in all eras and all branches of the U.S. Armed Forces. A popular parade for nearly a decade, the parade is held the Saturday before the official Veterans Day (November 11). Join the thousands of flag-waving spectators who line Atlantic Blvd to watch the marchers stream by: high school bands, military units, fire department vehicles, police officers, proud veterans and families. The parade kicks off about 10AM from Harding Street to 56th Street then loops back. Afterwards, head to the Long Beach Vietnam Veterans Memorial at Houghton Park for a ceremony and patriotic concert by the Long Beach Junior Concert Band. You can't miss the memorial— a real Huey helicopter used in Vietnam War combat is part of the statuary.

WHEN: Sat before Veterans Day (Nov 11)
PARKING: FREE on side streets east and west of Atlantic Blvd
THOMAS GUIDE: 765 E1
KID-FRIENDLY * WHEELCHAIR/STROLLER ACCESS

Main Street Canoga Park's Dia de Los Muertos

SHERMAN WAY
Between Canoga and Jordan Aves, Canoga Park 91303
818-346-4892
www.mainstreetcanogapark.org

Honor departed loved ones during the traditional festivities of The Day of the Dead, held on All Soul's Day, November 2. Enter the altar contest by designing a memorial to your ancestors. Discover design tips for next year's contest with cultural arts & crafts workshops. Entertainment includes Madrid Theatre performances, flamenco dancers and music for the soul. Join the traditional remembrance procession to Our Lady of the Valley Catholic Church, which closes the daylong fest.

WHEN: All Soul's Day, Nov. 2
PARKING: Metered street * **THOMAS GUIDE:** 530 A5
KID-FRIENDLY * WHEELCHAIR/STROLLER ACCESS

Music Center Family Festival

MUSIC CENTER
135 N Grand Ave, LA 90012
213-250-ARTS
www.musicenter.org

Bring your youngsters to LA's creative core and help them find their creative center, too. Held in early November on the center's outdoor plaza, the fest is a celebration of music, dance, art, and the human imagination. Live contemporary, jazz, and world music expose kids to sounds they won't hear on rock radio while dance performances give them a close-up look at an art form they may have only seen on TV. At the story-telling tent, master yarn-spinners tell tales that will fascinate the entire family. Art-making workshops provide instruction and materials for kids to make fun projects, which at past festivals have included animal masks, bird puppets, sand paintings, and spiral sculptures. A dozen or so downtown restaurants have booths set up to sell tasting portions of their delicacies for $5 or less.

WHEN: Early Nov
PARKING: Pay garage (nearby lots and structures may be less expensive)
THOMAS GUIDE: 634 F3
KID-FRIENDLY * WHEELCHAIR/STROLLER ACCESS

Native Voices at the Autry Festival of Plays

MUSEUM OF THE AMERICAN WEST
4700 Western Heritage Way, LA 90027
323-667-2000
www.autry-museum.org

Reserve your seats now for some of the best-staged productions by Native American playwrights and directors. As part of the museum's Native Voices program, three new works by established Native American playwrights are produced as readings for the Wells Fargo Theatre. The members of the productions represent diverse Native American tribes from Apache to Métis to Taos to Choctaw. While attendance is FREE, guests are encouraged to donate a non-perishable food item.

WHEN: Fri – Sun in Nov, dates vary
PARKING: FREE * **THOMAS GUIDE:** 564 B4
WHEELCHAIR ACCESS

Pasadena Doo Dah Parade

OLD PASADENA
Raymond Ave & Holly St, Pasadena 91103
626-440-7379
www.pasadenadoodahparade.com

Okay, so it's not the Tournament of Roses. However, when was the last time the Rose Parade had Claude Rains & the 20-Man Memorial Invisible Man Marching Drill Team? Or how about the BBQ & Hibachi Marching Grill Team? Teeming with social and political satire, this off-the-wall event has been strolling the streets of Old Pasadena's historic district for close to three decades. About 1,500 participants in 100 marching groups wearing outrageous costumes and utilizing unusual props, strut past the 45,000 spectators. Look for these themed marchers: Bungee Barbies, Dead Rose Queens and the Howdy Krishnas. You get the drift. Held the last Sunday before Thanksgiving, the parade starts at 11:30AM, rain or shine, at Raymond Avenue and Holly Street. Be forewarned: some parade humor might be offensive to parents with young children.

WHEN: 11:30AM, last Sun before Thanksgiving
PARKING: Pay structures located along the parade route
THOMAS GUIDE: 565 H4

Santa Clarita Marathon

FINISH LINE: NEWHALL PARK
24923 Newhall Ave, Newhall 91321
888-823-3455 or 661-259-2489
www.scmarathon.org

Get ready, get set and go to the Santa Clarita Marathon the first Sunday in November, where runners can qualify for the Boston Marathon. Though competitors pay an entry fee, spectators get their adrenal rush from the sidelines and enjoy the day's entertainment and festivities for FREE. The main marathon kicks off near Lang Station and Soledad Canyon Roads in Canyon Country, with runners crossing the finish line at Newhall Park in Newhall. The race route traverses area streets, paved trails and *paseos* through the Santa Clarita Valley communities of Saugus, Canyon Country, Valencia and Newhall. The park is also the site of the marathon festival filled with vendor booths, children's activities, musical entertainment and an awards presenta-tion. In addition to the qualifying marathon, spectators can watch the half marathon, the 5K and a Kid K Fun Run.

WHEN: 1st Sun in Nov
PARKING: FREE school lots, street * **THOMAS GUIDE:** 4550 H7
KID-FRIENDLY * **WHEELCHAIR/STROLLER ACCESS**

Snow Day Extravaganza

HANSEN DAM SPORTS CENTER
11770 Foothill Blvd, Lake View Terrace 91342
www.laparks.org

The weather forecast is snow for the Northeast San Fernando Valley as 100 tons of the cold stuff descends on the sports center. Choose from three different snow play-grounds including a sledding area and remember to dress properly for the frosty event. Even though snow day happens before Thanksgiving, Santa Claus makes an appearance in this local winter wonderland. Children's holiday karaoke, community information booths and other activities included.

WHEN: Late Nov
PARKING: FREE * **THOMAS GUIDE:** 502 G2
KID-FRIENDLY * **WHEELCHAIR/STROLLER ACCESS**

Thanksgiving Dinner at the LA Mission

LOS ANGELES MISSION
303 E 5th St, LA 90013
213-629-1227
www.losangelesmission.org

Volunteering to serve a FREE meal to homeless families and individuals is not as easy as it sounds. About 5,000 people will be served hot turkey with all the trimmings the day before the official national Thanksgiving holiday and it takes 400 helpers to do it. Reserve a time weeks in advance for the serving line since this charitable event is a popular way to give to those in need. You may even get to rub elbows with celebrity servers. Consider donating cash so others without can enjoy this special holiday meal for FREE.

WHEN: Wed before Thanksgiving
PARKING: Pay lots, metered street * **THOMAS GUIDE:** 634 F5

DECEMBER

Black Doll Exhibition

WILLIAM GRANT STILL ARTS CENTER
2520 West View St, LA 90016
323-734-1164
www.fowgs.org

Discover the artistry and creativity of dolls at this annual exhibit that's been showcasing black versions of this universal symbol of humankind for almost 25 years. Begun in response to a social experiment that showed African-American children choosing white dolls over black ones, the exhibit has featured thousands of black dolls over the years from antique and collectibles to those designed and crafted by contemporary artists. The result is an exhibit that highlights how ordinary playthings can be quite extraordinary.

WHEN: mid-Dec through Feb
PARKING: FREE * **THOMAS GUIDE:** 633 D6
KID-FRIENDLY * **WHEELCHAIR/STROLLER ACCESS**

Free Museum Admission on Christmas Day

SKIRBALL CULTURAL CENTER
2701 N Sepulveda Blvd, LA 90049
310-440-4500
www.skirball.org

Name one cultural institution open in LA on December 25. Okay, the above information gave it away. It's the Skirball, a museum that covers every facet of Jewish life and yet seeks to inspire and embrace people of all ethnic and cultural backgrounds. Discover something new, explore biblical times, take a tour. Bring the kids too; the museum provides FREE gallery kits with games and puzzles.

WHEN: Dec 25 & Dec 26
PARKING: $5 lot ★ **THOMAS GUIDE:** 591 F1
KID-FRIENDLY ★ **WHEELCHAIR/STROLLER ACCESS**

Ringing of the Korean Bell

ANGEL'S GATE PARK
3701 S Gaffey St, San Pedro 90731
310-548-7705
www.sanpedrochamber.com

While LA is hard-pressed to have a New Year's Celebration similar to New York City or Las Vegas, it does have a more literal ringing in of the New Year. Tucked away in Angel's Gate Park is a functioning copper bell that was donated in 1976 to the people of LA by the people of the Republic of Korea. Weighing in at 17 tons, the Korean Bell of Friendship is set in a stone pagoda-style building that looks out over the Pacific Ocean. As the clock strikes Midnight a wooden log is used to release the bell's welcoming sounds. The bell is struck only two other times each year: July 4, US Independence Day and August 15, Korean Independence Day.

WHEN: New Year's Eve, Dec 31
PARKING: FREE * **THOMAS GUIDE:** 854 B2
KID-FRIENDLY * HISTORIC * WHEELCHAIR/STROLLER ACCESS

Snow Zone

PERSHING SQUARE

532 S Olive St, LA 90013
213-847-4970
www.laparks.org

Downtown LA becomes a snow playground when tons of frosty flakes drop in on Pershing Square. The mountain of snow is expected to last only four hours, so put your warm mittens on early. Frozen fun includes virtual snow games, a remote control "teeny weeny zambeeny," arts & crafts, and a live musical performance sponsored by Radio Disney. Some activities charge a fee.

WHEN: Sat, date varies
PARKING: Underground, $4 all day * **THOMAS GUIDE:** 634 E4
KID-FRIENDLY * WHEELCHAIR/STROLLER ACCESS

Tournament of Roses Parade Float Decorating

TOURNAMENT OF ROSES HOUSE

391 S Orange Grove Blvd, Pasadena 91184
626-449-4100
www.tournamentofroses.com

Take part in one of the most-watched parades on Earth by signing up to decorate a Tournament of Roses Parade float. While most floats have become technologically sophisticated with computerized and motorized moving parts, they still must be hand-decorated using only flowers, plants, seeds, leaves and other botanicals. One Rose Parade float will use more flowers than the average florist will in five years. To sign up, visit the Rose Parade Web site to contact major float builders and local organizations constructing their own.

WHEN: Dec 26 to Dec 31
PARKING: Varies * **THOMAS GUIDE:** Varies

Note
FIND MORE
DECEMBER EVENTS
UNDER WINTER
HOLIDAYS
*

Holiday Events

Chinese New Year's Festival

CHINATOWN
N Hill St & Central Plaza, LA 90012
213-680-0243
www.chinatownla.com

Celebrate the New Year—Chinese-style—near the first
new moon of the year based on the ancient Chinese calendar. Be sure to see the 100+ year-old LA Golden Dragon
Parade on Broadway Saturday afternoon (See separate
event this chapter). A bounty of Chinese and Asian entertainment highlights this two-day festival dedicated to the
Lunar New Year including cultural and performing arts
from opera to lion dances to acrobatics. Watch martial arts
demonstrations, shadow puppet performances and magic
shows, all for FREE on the Central Plaza.

WHEN: Sat – Sun in Jan or Feb, dates vary
PARKING: Varies * **THOMAS GUIDE:** 634 H2
KID-FRIENDLY * **WHEELCHAIR/STROLLER ACCESS**

Golden Dragon Parade

CHINATOWN
900 to 1000 N Broadway, LA 90012
213-680-0243
www.lagoldendragonparade.com

Start the New Year right by scaring off evil spirits when you attend one of oldest Lunar New Year parades in the US. The procession is populated with the colorful Chinese dragons that weave through the parade route. Sometimes manned by up to 20 performers, the dragons keep bad karma away. Also stepping off for the parade down Broadway are marching bands, Chinese acrobats, Miss L.A. Chinatown Queen and her court, elaborate floats and civic groups. Past Grand Marshals have included actress Ming Na (*ER* and *The Joy Luck Club*) and Norm Chow, offensive coordinator for the USC Trojans. Entertaining LA spectators for 100+ years, the parade attracts about 40,000 onlookers. Parking is tough. Best bet is to park elsewhere and take the Metro Gold Line to Chinatown.

WHEN: Sat afternoon in Jan or Feb, date varies
PARKING: Varies * **THOMAS GUIDE:** 634 H2
KID-FRIENDLY * **WHEELCHAIR/STROLLER ACCESS**

Hollywood Lunar New Year Parade & Festival

HOLLYWOOD BOULEVARD
Between Vermont Ave & Hobart Blvd, Hollywood 90027
310-442-2712 (parade hotline)
www.kscitv.com

Get in the New Year groove Hollywood-style and celebrate tinsel town's version of Lunar New Year. Sponsored by KSCI-TV, Southern California's multi-language station, the parade sweeps down Hollywood Boulevard between

Vermont Avenue and Hobart Boulevard. Look for Chinese lion dancers, marching bands and floats. This being Hollywood there are several Asian celebrities to juice up the crowd. Past celebs have included Brook Lee, Miss Universe '97; popular Vietnamese singers My Huyen and Paolo; Filipino superstar Gary V.; and actors Garret Wang from *Star Trek* and John Cho from the movie, *American Pie*. The celebration continues with a festival on the boulevard between Western Avenue and Hobart Boulevard.

WHEN: Sat in Jan or Feb, date varies
PARKING: Pay lots, metered street * **THOMAS GUIDE:** 594 A4
KID-FRIENDLY

LA Tet Festival

WHITTIER NARROWS REGIONAL PARK
1000 N Durfee Ave, LA 90660
626-571-2641
www.latetfest.net

Wear red for good fortune at this Vietnamese Lunar New Year celebration. Tet, a word symbolic of joy that's shared with family and friends, also represents a time to reunite Vietnamese Americans with their ethnic roots. Tet officially begins on the first day of the Lunar New Year and last seven days. Join 50,000 visitors to watch lion and dragon dances, listen to Asian music performances and see the crowning of Miss and Mrs. LA Tet. There's more: orchid and bonsai exhibits, children's traditional costume contest and a karaoke contest. Bring extra cash for carnival rides and food.

WHEN: Sat – Sun in Jan or Feb, dates vary
PARKING: Varies * **THOMAS GUIDE:** 636 J5
KID-FRIENDLY

San Gabriel Valley Lunar New Year Festival

VALLEY BOULEVARD

Between Garfield & Chapel Aves, Alhambra 91801

626-284-1234

www.lunarnewyearparade.com

Celebrate Lunar New Year in one of the largest Chinese-American commercial districts in Southern California. An outreach event as well as a cultural one, the one-day festival includes 150+ booths featuring local and national companies, community groups and vendors. About 50,000 people head to the district to listen and watch the FREE entertainment on two stages and peruse the fest's Cultural Village exhibits. Bored with traditional festival entertainment? Pause to watch great minds at work during the youth chess tournaments.

WHEN: Sat in Jan or Feb, date varies
PARKING: Varies * **THOMAS GUIDE:** 596 C5
KID-FRIENDLY

San Gabriel Valley Lunar New Year Parade

VALLEY BOULEVARD

From Del Mar Ave, San Gabriel to Chapel Ave, Alhambra 91801

626-284-1234

www.lunarnewyearparade.com

Bring yourself good luck by attending this popular Lunar New Year parade that winds 1.5 miles through the heart of the San Gabriel Valley. Golden dragons, lion dancers and martial arts acrobats all take turns marching past and entertaining the crowd of 30,000 that lines Valley Boulevard for the annual procession. The spirit of the parade, embraced by the decorated floats and bouncing marching bands, is broadcast on the Chinese radio station, KMNY1370 AM. Sponsored by the cities of San Gabriel & Alhambra.

WHEN: Sat in Jan or Feb, date varies
PARKING: Varies ＊ **THOMAS GUIDE:** 596 C7
KID-FRIENDLY

EARTH DAY EVENTS

Arbor Day Celebration

SUN VALLEY RECREATION CENTER
8133 Vineland Ave, Sun Valley 91352
888-LA-PARKS or 213-473-7089
www.laparks.org

Hug a tree and hug Smokey the Bear at the LA City of Park & Recreation Department's annual Arbor Day/Earth Day celebration. Take advantage of the FREE workshops on tree planting and tree care, look for tree giveaways. With the focus on trees, the event features forestry demonstrations of tree and speed pole climbing and cross cut and chain sawing. FREE arts & crafts for kids, live music and other activities. Co-sponsored by the LA Department of Water & Power and the city's Public Works Department.

WHEN: Sat in Apr, date varies
PARKING: FREE ＊ **THOMAS GUIDE:** 532 J2
KID-FRIENDLY ＊ **WHEELCHAIR/STROLLER ACCESS**

Celebration in Honor of Earth Day

CHATSWORTH NATURE PRESERVE
Valley Circle Blvd & Box Canyon Rd, Chatsworth 91304
818-769-1521
www.sanfernandovalleyaudubon.org/sfvas/

Relax under the shade of 100-year-old oak trees and tour a nature preserve that's rarely open to the public at this annual Earth-honoring event. The 1,400-acre Chatsworth Nature Preserve is an environmental oasis for wildlife and a stopping point for Canadian Geese during their migrations. Owned by the Department of Water & Power, the land has been kept at bay from developers and is considered a sacred place by many. Greet the beginning of Earth Month —a month-long celebration in place of Earth Day—by watching the dances and listening to the legends of Chumash and Tongva Indian tribes. Talk with members of several earth-friendly groups including the Sierra Club, the Canada Goose Project, the Wishtoyo Foundation (Chumash) and the San Fernando Valley Audubon Society. Bring water, food, blankets to sit on and a camera for memories. No parking, no smoking inside the preserve.

WHEN: 1st Sun in Earth Month (Apr)
PARKING: FREE on streets * **THOMAS GUIDE:** 529 E1
KID-FRIENDLY

Children's Earth Day at Star-Eco Station

STAR-ECO STATION
10101 W Jefferson Blvd, Culver City 90232
310-842-8060
www.ecostation.org

Join 15,000 eco-friendly folks at one of the hippest places to learn about planet Earth. This environmental science and exotic wildlife rescue center's annual outdoor fest was named "the Best Earth Day Celebration" in a local poll. Learn about and celebrate the Earth with plenty of hands-on activities and games for kids. Go on brief guided tours of La Ballona Creek. FREE stuff handed out at booths featuring environmental groups such as Heal the Bay, the Santa Monica Baykeepers and U.S. Fish & Wildlife. This is Star-Eco Station's only FREE event.

WHEN: Sun, late Apr, date varies
PARKING: FREE in nearby lots; FREE shuttle * **THOMAS GUIDE:** 672 H2
KID-FRIENDLY

Earth Day at the SEA Laboratory

SEA LAB
1021 N Harbor Dr, Redondo Beach 90277
310-318-7458
www.redondo.org

Dive in to this earth-friendly outreach festival at this marine education center on the edge of King Harbor that's a program of the LA Conservation Corps. Have close encounters with marine animals, learn how to save the shore and help preserve the beach by cleaning it up. Take a FREE tour of the SEA Lab's aquariums, enter the amateur sand sculpture contest and participate in FREE games. Make new environmentally conscious friends at the educational booths.

WHEN: Sat in Apr, date varies
PARKING: FREE at Camacho's Restaurant 655 N Harbor Dr
THOMAS GUIDE: 762 H4
KID-FRIENDLY

Earth Day Celebration

KEN MALLOY REGIONAL HARBOR PARK

25820 Vermont Ave, LA 90744

888-LA-PARKS or 310-548-7728

www.laparks.org

Show support for this Harbor area park's 70-acre lake by attending this FREE Earth Day Celebration featuring a Save the Lake relay race. Teams of four in canoes compete in short races; the cost to compete is $40, which goes to the Save the Lake Fund; spectators get to watch the races for FREE. Explore nature and wildlife exhibits from the Audubon Society, the Cabrillo Marine Aquarium, the Marine Mammal Center and other groups. Shake hands with Smokey the Bear, go on bird-watching walks and attend workshops.

WHEN: Sat in Apr, date varies
PARKING: FREE * **THOMAS GUIDE:** 794 A6
KID-FRIENDLY * **WHEELCHAIR/STROLLER ACCESS**

Earth Day Fair at Cabrillo Marine Aquarium

CABRILLO MARINE AQUARIUM

3720 Stephen White Dr, San Pedro 90731

310-548-7562

www.cabrilloaq.org

Cleanup the oceans of our planet—or at least part of one—at the aquarium's annual beachy trash pick-up and Earth Day celebration. Hit the sand and surf in the morning to help restore the shore then stay for the fun fair. Join FREE guide walks to the Salinas de San Pedro, the adjacent salt marsh and visit the aquarium for FREE. Several eco-friendly activities for kids and 40+ environmental groups on hand offering FREE information. Vendors sell food, ecology books and environmental products.

WHEN: Sat in Apr, date varies
PARKING: $7 per car for beach lot or park elsewhere and take the trolley
THOMAS GUIDE: 854 C2
KID-FRIENDLY ∗ **WHEELCHAIR/STROLLER ACCESS**

Earth Day on the Promenade

SANTA MONICA'S THIRD STREET PROMENADE
Between Broadway & Wilshire Blvd, Santa Monica 90403
888-295-8372
www.EarthDayLA.org

Be a friend of the Earth at one of the West's biggest Eco-fests. About 20,000 environmentally concerned citizens converge on Earth Day LA's tribute to ecology-friendly lifestyles. The three-block promenade between Broadway and Wilshire includes 60 ecology exhibits and a solar powered stage featuring the Sustainability Awards, environmental speakers and eclectic World Music performers. Check out Toyota Prius hybrid vehicles, energy efficient appliances and solar energy products. Learn about hemp and organic cotton clothing, play Earth Tic-Tac-Toe and visit with exotic wildlife. Purchase wholesome food at the Whole Foods Markets pavilion. Learn how you can save the Earth from the dozens of top LA and national environmental organizations including Heal the Bay, TreePeople and the Sierra Club.

WHEN: Sat in Apr, date varies
PARKING: $7 all day in parking garages ∗ **THOMAS GUIDE:** 671 D1
KID-FRIENDLY ∗ **WHEELCHAIR/STROLLER ACCESSIBLE**

Earth Day with the Friends of Madrona Marsh

MADRONA MARSH NATURE CENTER

3201 Plaza del Amo, Torrance 90503

310-782-3989

www.friendsofmadronamarsh.com

Help restore and clean up this rare Southern California vernal marsh preserve on a former oil-drilling site. Wear sturdy shoes and work gloves and assist in clearing the remains of roads, railroad tracks and debris. A natural depression that becomes a wetland during the rainy season, the marsh is a city haven for more than 250 bird species and for the endangered El Segundo Blue Butterfly and Palos Verdes Blue Butterfly. As the only vernal marsh left in LA County, the preserve serves as an educational example of habitat restoration. All ages and skills welcome. Tools and refreshments provided. Meet at the nature center across the street from the preserve. After the morning clean up stay for the free docent-led nature walk.

WHEN: Sat in Apr, date varies
PARKING: FREE * **THOMAS GUIDE:** 763 E7

Eco-Maya Festival

BARNSDALL ART PARK

4800 Hollywood Blvd, Hollywood 90027

323-644-6269

www.ecomayafestival.com

Focus on Maya culture, heritage and the ecology of the Maya territories at this popular Mother Earth Day Celebration. Now a decade old, the two-day fest is a showcase for Maya traditions that attracts 15,000 festival goers. Among the highlights: the cooking of the largest tamal (tamale) in the world, the largest gathering of

Marimba performers, the Mesoamerican International Film and Video Festival, Para los Ninos (a space for kids), arts & crafts fair, folklorico dancers, rock en Espanol performers and an Art and Spoken Word exhibit. Entrance on Hollywood Blvd.

WHEN: Sat – Sun in Apr, dates vary
PARKING: At the Kaiser lot * **THOMAS GUIDE:** 593 G4
KID-FRIENDLY * **WHEELCHAIR/STROLLER ACCESS**

Greening the Earth

MEMORIAL PARK
Raymond Ave & Walnut St, Pasadena 91103
626-744-4755
www.ci.pasadena.ca.us

Tune in to nature's harmony: water wise landscaping, backyard composting, vermicomposting (with worms!). Learn friendly tree care and how to create a spring garden. Chat up energy-saving experts and recycling mavens at the event hosted by the Pasadena Water & Power and the city Public Works Department. Hob nob with garden club folks and talk with members of native plant societies. FREE conservation goodies! FREE hourly how-to workshops. Green thumbs, green earth.

WHEN: Sat in Apr, date varies
PARKING: FREE * **THOMAS GUIDE:** 565 H4
KID-FRIENDLY * **WHEELCHAIR/STROLLER ACCESS**

Cinco de Mayo at Olvera Street

EL PUEBLO DE LOS ANGELES HISTORIC MONUMENT
125 Paseo de la Plaza, LA 90012
213-625-5045
www.olvera-street.com
www.ci.la.ca.us/ELP/

Celebrate the historic battle of Puebla, a small town in Mexico whose poorly equipped soldiers managed to defeat French troops on May 5, 1862. Often mistaken for Mexican Independence Day (Sept 16), Cinco de Mayo is a celebration of Mexican-American heritage. The FREE three-day fiesta at the monument's Olvera Street marketplace features mariachis, flamenco dancers and ballet folklorico. Learn about Mexico's history at several cultural workshops and let the kids break piñatas. Live music, colorful costumes and an exhibit of Mexican dresses.

WHEN: Fri – Sun, on or before May 5
PARKING: Pay lots, metered street * **THOMAS GUIDE:** 634 G3
KID-FRIENDLY * **WHEELCHAIR/STROLLER ACCESS**

Fiesta Broadway LA

DOWNTOWN LA
Broadway between 11th & Temple Sts, LA 90012
310-914-0015
www.fiestabroadway.la

Salsa, Samba and Tango over to Fiesta Broadway LA, a grande festival of Latino musical artists that draws 500,000 revelers. What began as a musical showcase of Latin music has become the largest Cinco de Mayo celebration in the world—despite being held on an April Sunday. For six hours the area pulsates with musical stars such as Tito Puente, Celia Cruz, Jose Feliciano and Paulina Rubio. To accommodate the four concert stages, the 150+ vendor booths and the crowds, 36 square blocks of Downtown LA are cordoned off for the FREE fiesta. Broadway is the center of the action between 11th & Temple Sts and Olive & Main Sts. Sponsored by McDonald's and presented by Albertsons, the fiesta draws big name companies such as Home Depot, Kohl's & Pepsi who sponsor family fun zones, activity booths and major pavilions featuring autos, fashion and food.

WHEN: Sunday before May 5, date varies
PARKING: Varies * **THOMAS GUIDE:** 634 E5/G3
KID-FRIENDLY * **WHEELCHAIR/STROLLER ACCESS**

Target Arts Live!
Cinco de Mayo Celebration

MADRID THEATRE
21622 Sherman Way, Canoga Park 91303
818-347-9938
www.madridtheatre.org

Kick off this cultural theatre's yearlong performing arts series with a FREE Cinco de Mayo celebration. Sponsored by the City of Los Angeles Cultural Affairs Department &

Target Corporation, the festive performances include Latin music and mariachis. Create Mexican-inspired crafts at the FREE hands-on workshops afterwards. A former run-down adult movie house, the Madrid Theatre is a prime example of bringing arts back into the community. Located at the heart of historic Antique Row in downtown Canoga Park, the 450-seat theatre is the San Fernando Valley's largest live, professional-level performing arts facility.

WHEN: Sun on or before May 5
PARKING: Metered street * **THOMAS GUIDE:** 530 A5
KID-FRIENDLY * **WHEELCHAIR ACCESS**

Long Beach Cinco de Mayo

CHITTICK FIELD
Walnut Ave & Pacific Coast Hwy (HWY 1), Long Beach 90813
562-436-8593 (festival) 562-570-1725 (park)
www.longbeachcincodemayo.com

Viva Mexico! at this three-day FREE community fiesta. The salsa is hot and so is the music from mariachis to reggae to punta. Watch ballet folklorico, Aztec dancers and Mexican stars on two entertainment stages. Visit 100+ booths featuring community resources, business expo, health faire and arts & crafts. The FREE Dia de Los Ninos, a children's day area, keeps kids busy and so will 30+ carnival rides for a nominal fee. Meet the Miss Cinco de Mayo Queen, root for the players in a soccer tournament and enter an essay contest. About 50,000 visitors attend the fiesta sponsored by the Latino Business Community Educational Center, the Long Beach Department of Parks, Recreation & Marine and St. Mary Medical Center.

WHEN: Fri – Sun on or before May 5
PARKING: FREE at Pacific Coast Campus-Long Beach City College, entrance on PCH; Butler Elementary School and Universal Care lot, 1/2 block from the event
THOMAS GUIDE: 795 G5
KID-FRIENDLY * **WHEELCHAIR/STROLLER ACCESS**

Universal CityWalk's Cinco de Mayo Celebration

1000 Universal Center Dr, Universal City 91608
818-622-4455
www.citywalkhollywood.com

Salsa to the sounds of FREE Latin music during CityWalk's spin on Cinco de Mayo. The thematic shopping & entertainment park's stage rumbles with sizzling sounds for the evening crowds. Rumba to the musical celebration for FREE or slip into the Rumba Room, CityWalk's popular multi-level Latin nightclub for the 21+ club crowd. While the club charges an admission fee most nights, Sundays are FREE with FREE salsa lessons starting at 8PM.

WHEN: May 5 evening hours
PARKING: $8 * **THOMAS GUIDE:** 563 C7

FOURTH OF JULY

Alhambra July 4th Celebration

ALMANSOR PARK
800 S Almansor St, Alhambra 91801
626-570-5081
www.cityofalhambra.org

Raise the flag and raise your spirits at this home-style Independence Day celebration. Perfect for families and kids, the city's Parks & Recreation Department hosts this afternoon of mini-carnival games, crafts and contests. Bring a picnic lunch and snacks or purchase traditional festival eats and treats from vendors. The event also features a dog show but no family pets, including dogs, may attend. Enjoy the FREE music and stay for the 25-minute sky-illuminating show.

WHEN: July 4th afternoon
PARKING: FREE ✶ **THOMAS GUIDE:** 596 C6
KID-FRIENDLY ✶ **WHEELCHAIR/STROLLER ACCESS**

Angels Gate Park Fourth of July

ANGELS GATE PARK
3601 S Gaffey St, San Pedro 90731
888-LA-PARKS or 310-548-7705
www.laparks.org

Begin the celebration of Independence Day with the traditional bell ringing ceremony at the *Korean Friendship Bell,* located in a pagoda-style building inside the park. The massive bell is rung using a log and is done only on America's Independence Day, Korean Independence Day (Aug 15) and New Year's Eve. Hang out in the park that has incredible views of the Pacific Ocean and Catalina Island. Fix-up a picnic or purchase hot dogs and hamburgers. For kids ages 3 to 5, there's a tyke bike parade so decorate their wheelers at home and bring them for the procession. Watch kite flying or bring your own. Stay for the fireworks that brilliantly burst over nearby Cabrillo Beach. If there's no fog, you'll also see the pyrotechnics show at the Queen Mary in Long Beach.

WHEN: July 4th; fireworks at 9PM
PARKING: tktktk * **THOMAS GUIDE:** 854 B2
KID-FRIENDLY * **WHEELCHAIR/STROLLER ACCESS**

Anniversary of the First Independence Day Celebration in LA

FORT MOORE PIONEER MEMORIAL
451 N Hill Street, LA 90012
www.olvera-street.com

Discover how Angelenos acknowledged the first Independence Day in LA during this all day celebration at the Fort Moore Pioneer Memorial. Built by the Mormon

Battalion during the war with Mexico, Fort Moore stood on the hill above El Pueblo de Los Angeles. On July 4th 1847, US troops raised the flag of the United States here. Although the fort was demolished and the land turned into a playground, the largest bas-relief military monument in the US commemorates it. Witness the only cannon and musket fire salute for the Fourth. FREE activities include historical re-enactments, outdoor dance and balloons for kids. Some entertainment held down the hill on Olvera Street.

WHEN: July 4th
PARKING: FREE at LA Unified School District offices, 450 N Grand Ave
THOMAS GUIDE: 634 G3
KID-FRIENDLY

July 4 Fireworks Extravaganza

BURTON CHACE PARK
13650 Mindanao Way, Marina Del Rey 90292
310-305-9545
www.beaches.co.la.ca.us

Pyrotechnics pulsate over Marina del Rey's main channel during the annual fireworks show that's choreographed to patriotic music. While John Souza's (symphony) booms, the fireworks plume over the water. The best place to watch the sky show is at Burton Chace Park. Hear the music broadcast in syc on FM radio KXLU 88.9 or relayed over loudspeakers at the park. Sponsored by the Los Angeles County Department of Beaches and Harbors.

WHEN: 9PM July 4th
PARKING: County beach lots * **THOMAS GUIDE:** 672 B7
KID-FRIENDLY

Palmdale Fourth of July Celebration

PALMDALE HIGH SCHOOL
2137 East Avenue R, Palmdale 93550
661-267-5611 (City of Palmdale)
www.cityofpalmdale.org

Join the throngs of people who descend upon Palmdale every July 4 for a panoramic view of the increasingly popular Independence Day fireworks light show. The City of Palmdale, usually in collaboration with Waste Management of Antelope Valley and various other community agencies and businesses, sponsor what has been called "Antelope Valley's largest fireworks spectacular." See the sky above Palmdale sparkle with streaks of red, white, blue and green—a vision that surely heightens the sense of patriotic pride among spectators. Let the rhythm of American tunes, performed by a live band, capture your holiday spirit and set your adrenal flowing. Vendors sell beverages and snacks. Early arrival is recommended. Gates open at 6:30PM, musical entertainment starts at 7:30PM.

WHEN: July 4th
PARKING: Call for information ∗ **THOMAS GUIDE:** 4286 E2
KID-FRIENDLY ∗ **WHEELCHAIR/STROLLER ACCESS**

Rancho Palos Verdes Independence Day Celebration

PT. VICENTE PARK/CIVIC CENTER
30940 Hawthorne Blvd, Rancho Palos Verdes 90275
310-544-5260
www.palosverdes.com/rpv/recreationparks/

Juice up your lips and rev up your hips for a pie-eating, hoola hooping old-fashioned Fourth of July celebration. Greet Uncle Sam wearing his red, white and blue top hat as he circles the celebration on stilts. Get into the community spirit by visiting dozens of local civic information booths. Ride a pony, feed some cuties at the petting zoo and watch the dog acts and obedience training demonstrations. Shop for arts & crafts, play carnival-style games and even take a real helicopter ride (for a fee).

WHEN: July 4th
PARKING: $2 per vehicle for on-site parking; FREE shuttle service along Hawthorne Blvd between Ralphs Market and Golden Cove Center
THOMAS GUIDE: 822 G4
KID-FRIENDLY ∗ **WHEELCHAIR/STROLLER ACCESS**

Santa Clarita Fourth of July Celebration

NEWHALL PARK
24933 Newhall Ave, Santa Clarita 91321
661-255-4910
www.santa-clarita.com

Celebrate the nation's birthday with a Santa Clarita tradition that dates back to 1932—the annual Independence Day Parade. Considered one of the grandest Fourth of July parades in the country, with its wide array of floats, marching bands and honored guests, the event draws several thousand participants each year. The day actually kicks off about 7AM with a Rotary Club pancake breakfast followed by a 5K run down the parade route. Once the parade ends, spectators congregate in Newhall Park to enjoy a four-hour concert from 11AM to 3PM., which features both professional and student musicians. Anticipation mounts as crowds await the spectacular fireworks display, hosted by Santa Clarita City Hall at 9:30PM over the Valencia Town Center Mall. The sparkling pyrotechnics are visible for miles around.

WHEN: July 4th
PARKING: Call for information ∗ **THOMAS GUIDE:** 4550 H7
KID-FRIENDLY ∗ **WHEELCHAIR/STROLLER ACCESS**

Sierra Madre Fourth of July

MEMORIAL PARK

222 W Sierra Madre Blvd, Sierra Madre 91024

626-355-7135 (city of Sierra Madre)

www.sierramadre4thofjuly.us

Immerse yourself in the inescapable hometown feeling of patriotism and Americana. Celebrate over the weekend with FREE outdoor concerts, Dixieland music, an antique calliope show and movies in the park. There's a parade "where half the town marches and the other half watches," and a pre-parade party the night before. Enjoy the park's food booths and beer garden while savoring "Life, liberty, and the pursuit of happiness."

WHEN: On or near July 4th
PARKING: FREE ★ **THOMAS GUIDE:** 567 A2
KID-FRIENDLY ★ **WHEELCHAIR/STROLLER ACCESS**

Hansen Dam Fourth of July Spectacular

HANSEN DAM RECREATION AREA

11770 Foothill Blvd, Lakeview Terrace 91342

818-899-3779

www.hansen4th.com

Admire the celebration in the sky as the San Fernando Valley's largest fireworks display drapes the night in sparkling spirals and glittering bursts of color. The fireworks are the finale to the recreation area's all-day Fourth of July gathering featuring FREE concerts and entertainment, from ballet *folklorico* to line dancing to retro rock. Choreographed to patriotic music, the spectacular sky show is broadcast live on NBC4 and Telemundo 52. Bring a picnic or buy traditional July 4th food—BBQ corn, snow cones, hamburgers—from vendors. Come early to ensure a parking spot—25,000 folks show up for the 9PM fireworks.

WHEN: 10AM to 9PM, July 4th
PARKING: $3 per car all day, $5 per larger vehicle all day
THOMAS GUIDE: 502 G2/H1
KID-FRIENDLY * **WHEELCHAIR/STROLLER ACCESS**

Free Halloween Movie in the Park

WEST HOLLYWOOD PARK
647 N San Vicente Blvd, West Hollywood 90069
323-848-6534
www.weho.org

Go on an al fresco film frolic for some pre-Halloween night fun. The City of West Hollywood puts you in the mood for the haunted holiday and their upcoming raucous costume carnaval with a FREE spooky outdoor screening. Bring a blanket and a picnic dinner but leave the alcohol and pets at home. Past movies have included classics such as John Waters' "Hairspray," starring Divine.

WHEN: Evening before Halloween
PARKING: Permit parking, pay lots ★ **THOMAS GUIDE:** 592 H7

Ghost and Horror Night

UCLA HAMMER MUSEUM
10899 Wilshire Blvd, UCLA 90024
310-443-7000
www.hammer.ucla.edu

Even grownups love scary stories. Listen to the spookiest tales from a dozen literati at the UCLA Hammer Museum's annual Halloween tribute. Part of the New American Writing series held in Gallery 6. You might be in for a trick-or-treat or two as some of the guest artists present more than just a ghostly reading.

WHEN: Sun eve before Oct 31
PARKING: $7 on campus ∗ **THOMAS GUIDE:** 632 B3

Haute Dogs Howl'oween Parade & Costume Contest

LIVINGSTON PARK
Livingston Dr at Park Ave, Belmont Shore 90803
562-570-3125 (park)
www.hautedogs.org

Calling all haunted hounds for the annual Haute Dog Howl'oween Pooch Parade & Canine Charity Costume Contest. Dress your devil dogs in their spookiest costumes to compete for prizes like a year's supply of doggie dinners while helping support Long Beach-area charities. The howlin' good time costs $10 for each costumed canine but the spooky spectacle is FREE for spectators. About 400 primped pups parade from Park Avenue to Second Street while a few thousand people watch the 12-block procession of spoofed up pets. The $10 registration fee funds local charities. Afterwards, canines compete for designed-for-dogs contests such as bobbing for Howl'oweenies, a tail-wagging contest and naturally, a howling competition.

WHEN: Sun afternoon, before or on Halloween
PARKING: FREE on street around Livingston Park and on Second St; FREE in city lots off Second St every Sun
THOMAS GUIDE: 826 B1
KID-FRIENDLY * **WHEELCHAIR/STROLLER ACCESS**

Hallowed Haunting Grounds

4343 Babcock Ave, Studio City 91604
www.hauntinggrounds.org

"Commune with us this hallowed evening," at the spookiest haunted house in LA. So invites the talking statue that first materialized on the lawn of this ordinary home on Halloween 1973 and has appeared every Oct 31 since. The man behind the curtain, so to speak, is Gary Corb, Study City resident and fan of Disneyland's Haunted Mansion. So much so, that Corb created his own ghostly realm for Halloween. More mysterious than maniacal, more ghostly than ghoulish, the FREE "haunting grounds" offers a craftily creepy experience with no blood or gore. The sights and sounds may frighten very young or sensitive children. Pay a visit…if you dare!

WHEN: 7PM to Midnight, Oct 29 to Oct 31
PARKING: Street * **THOMAS GUIDE:** 562 F5
KID-FRIENDLY

Halloween Howl

CLARK RECREATION BUILDING
861 Valley Dr, Hermosa Beach 90254
310-318-0280
www.hermosabch.org

Head for a real old-fashioned Halloween event put on by local community groups. For kids ages 12 and under, the

"Howl" is really like a down-home party with treats and tricks for every young ghost and goblin. Come dressed in your spookiest garb for the costume parades, games booths and creepy crafts. FREE treats, a puppet show and a haunted house.

WHEN: Halloween evening
PARKING: FREE * **THOMAS GUIDE:** 762 H2
KID-FRIENDLY * **WHEELCHAIR/STROLLER ACCESS**

Intergenerational Pumpkin Carving Contest

PLUMMER PARK
7377 Santa Monica Blvd, West Hollywood 90046
323-848-6530
www.weho.org

Get the tips, tools and pumpkins you need at this ageless jack-o-lantern workshop. Seniors, teens and kids pool their creativity to carve the creepiest and funniest Halloween icons. After the two-hour carving event, the primed pumpkins are displayed at the West Hollywood Halloween Youth Carnaval. This fall FREEbie is one of several pre-Halloween night events leading up to the city's big bash—the Halloween Costume Carnaval.

WHEN: Fri before Halloween, date varies
PARKING: Permits, metered street, pay lots * **THOMAS GUIDE:** 593 C6
KID-FRIENDLY * **WHEELCHAIR/STROLLER ACCESS**

Kids' Halloween Costume Contest

WASHINGTON MUTUAL BANK (IN FRONT OF BUILDING)
5200 E Second St, Belmont Shore 90803
www.CommunityActionTeam.org

Dress up kids ages 12 and under for this fun, no strings attached, Halloween costume contest that could net them a cool $10 for their trick-or-treat bags. Ten contestants receive $10 each based on their costume's originality, creativity and appeal and all participants receive goodies like candy, stickers and kids' meal certificates. On-site registration is FREE but if you RSVP by e-mail (justinrudd@aol.com) at least 24-hours before the event, your costumed child will also receive a certificate of partic-ipation. Sponsored by the Community Action Team, an umbrella organization of events and programs designed to promote social wellbeing for the local community.

WHEN: Oct 30
PARKING: FREE on Second St, adjacent lots * **THOMAS GUIDE:** 826 B2
KID-FRIENDLY * **WHEELCHAIR/STROLLER ACCESS**

Mr. Bones Pumpkin Patch

10250 Wilshire Blvd, LA 90024
310-276-9827
www.mrbonespumpkinpatch.com

This tony side of town puts on country airs starting two weeks before All Hallows Eve. Bursting with bright orange orbs just waiting to turn into jack-o-lanterns, the tempo-rary pumpkin patch is delightfully farm-fresh with all the fall trimmings including cornstalks, Indian corn, gourds and straw bales. Don't like to scoop out squash? This sea-sonal sensation from Oregon provides the perfectly coifed pumpkin—carved or painted—and delivers it to your door. It's FREE to stroll through the countrified corner during the week; on weekends the nominal charge you pay can be applied to your pumpkin purchase.

WHEN: Oct 15 until Oct 31
PARKING: Metered street * **THOMAS GUIDE:** 632 D2
KID-FRIENDLY * **WHEELCHAIR/STROLLER ACCESS**

Trick or Treat At Belmont Shore

BELMONT SHORE

Second St between Bay Shore & Roycroft Aves, Long Beach 90803
562-434-3066
www.belmontshore.org

Trick or Treat at the beach for a safe Halloween outing before the sun goes down. A fun, no fright experience, little ghosts and goblins trot through the kid-friendly Belmont Shore neighborhood of merchants between 4PM and 6PM the night of All Hallows Eve. Look for bright orange pumpkins in the business windows and ask for a Halloween treat. Sponsored by the Belmont Shore Business Association.

WHEN: 4PM to 6PM, Halloween, Oct 31
PARKING: Pay lots * **THOMAS GUIDE:** 826 A1
KID-FRIENDLY * **WHEELCHAIR/STROLLER ACCESS**

Universal CityWalk Trick-or-Treat

UNIVERSAL CITYWALK

1000 Universal Center Dr, Universal City 91608
818-622-4455
www.citywalkhollywood.com

Are the kids ready to compete for 3,000 pounds of sweets? Then take them for a Hollywood-style trick-or-treat on the busiest block of blockbuster businesses. For more than three hours, all 65 stores hand out goodies to kids toting treat bags. Be sure to line up the costumed cuties (ages 0 to 12) for a contest mid-way through the sugar binge. Prizes awarded to different age groups and free digital photos available.

WHEN: Oct 31
PARKING: $7 * **THOMAS GUIDE:** 563 C7
KID-FRIENDLY * **WHEELCHAIR/STROLLER ACCESS**

West Hollywood Halloween Costume Carnaval

SANTA MONICA BLVD

between La Cienega Blvd & Doheny Dr,
West Hollywood 90069
323-848-6503
www.weho.org

Want to see a bearded 300-pound Dorothy Gale complete with blue gingham dress from the Wizard of Oz? Promenade, party or just gawk with nearly half a million other ghouls, goblins, movie star drag queens and other old souls in the ultimate Hollywood dress-up event. The annual phantasmagorical West Hollywood Halloween Costume Carnaval fills Santa Monica Blvd between La Cienega Blvd to Doheny Dr with gay and straight, young and old. The largest All Hallows Eve party in the nation, the outlandish street scene is preceded by a wicked week-long celebration featuring a FREE Friday afternoon intergenerational Pumpkin carving contest (sharpen those long claws), a FREE Saturday afternoon 50-yard "Drag" Race (dress in your outfit & heels), a Saturday evening youth Carnaval (bring those little monsters and a nominal entrance fee) and a FREE movie in West Hollywood Park. And don't miss the Sunday night The Red Dress Party benefit for AIDS (and put on plenty of rouge, Scarlett!!!)

WHEN: Carnaval, 6PM to Midnight, Oct 31;
dates vary for associated activities
PARKING: Permit parking suspended within West Hollywood city boundaries from 5PM Oct 31 to 7AM Nov 1.
FREE shuttle 5:30PM to 1:30AM between La Cienega Blvd & Fuller.
THOMAS GUIDE: 592 J6
KID-FRIENDLY * WHEELCHAIR/STROLLER ACCESS

WINTER HOLIDAYS

Christmas Tree Lane

SANTA ROSA AVENUE
Between Altadena Dr and Woodbury Ave, Altadena 91001
626-795-9311 (Pasadena Visitors & Convention Bureau)
www.pasadenacal.com

Experience history and holiday magic as you drive down
Christmas Tree Lane, a street lined with the tallest
Christmas trees this side of the North Pole. The 135 tower-
ing deodars were seedlings when the founders of Altadena
planted them in 1885. Area volunteers have been decorating the trees with 10,000 colorful bulbs since 1920, making it the oldest large-scale Christmas lighting exhibition
in Southern California. For full impact, be sure to start at
Altadena Drive and head south on the historic street, which
is listed in the California Historical Register.

WHEN: Mid-Dec to Jan 1
THOMAS GUIDE: 535 J6
KID-FRIENDLY

Downey Holiday Lane Parade

Downey Ave & Third St, Downey 90241
562-923-2191
www.downeychamber.com

Enjoy a holiday parade that's half a century old. Featuring a high profile grand marshal (aka celebrity or local politico) the parade gathers a spirited line up of participants and onlookers. Floats, marching bands, funky cars, equestrian units, politicians and school board members are all part of the festive procession. And don't forget Santa Claus! Riding with him on his float is the lucky winner of a raffle who gets to "Be A Star With Santa." Miss Downey and Miss Teen Downey ride in the parade and about 7,000 folks spend an early Sunday afternoon watching them and the parade go by.

WHEN: 1st Sun afternoon in Dec
PARKING: FREE * **THOMAS GUIDE:** 706 B5/C5
KID-FRIENDLY * **WHEELCHAIR/STROLLER ACCESS**

DWP Light Festival

GRIFFITH PARK
4730 Crystal Springs Dr, LA 90027
323-913-4688
www.dwplightfestival.com

Cruise the mile-long winter wonderland illuminating Griffith Park's Crystal Springs Drive starting the weekend before Thanksgiving and ending the day after Christmas. Hundreds of thousands of lights create 25 different sparkling displays that radiate a holiday spirit including a Christmas tree, a candy cane lane, the LA skyline, the famous Hollywood sign and a host of LA Zoo animals. A canopy of brilliance greets you at the entrance where you can donate an unwrapped gift to the LA Fire Department's toy drive. Half a million people visit the light display; a weeknight journey is less congested. As an alternative, bundle up and walk on the footpath or park in the zoo parking lot and take the FREE shuttle.

WHEN: 5PM to 10PM Fri before Thanksgiving to Fri after Christmas Day
PARKING: FREE in Zoo lot
SHUTTLE: FREE 7PM to 10PM daily during display
THOMAS GUIDE: 564 B4
KID-FRIENDLY * WHEELCHAIR/STROLLER ACCESS

Hollywood Christmas Parade

GRAUMAN'S CHINESE THEATER
6925 Hollywood Blvd, Hollywood 90028
323-962-8400
www.hollywoodspectacular.com

Gawk at real stars, not just symbolic ones imbedded in cement, at the annual holiday spectacular that floats down Hollywood Boulevard every Sunday after Thanksgiving. The Hollywood Chamber of Commerce rolls out the world's largest star-studded parade with celebrities from TV & film, the music industry, major sports teams and the North Pole. More than a million star-gazers and holiday well wishers turn out along the two-mile route that starts at the famous Grauman's Chinese Theater and is kicked off by the lighting of the new Kodak Theater's holiday tree. Marching bands, equestrian units, antique cars and floats cruise east along Hollywood Blvd, turning south on Vine St. and west on Sunset Blvd. The grand finale is the jolly old elf himself, Santa Claus, riding high on a sleigh with reindeer. The parade is FREE along the parade route but you can buy tickets for reserved ($35) and general admission ($25) grandstand seats. If you can't make it person, the parade is broadcast live on local KCAL-9 TV.

WHEN: Sunday after Thanksgiving
PARKING: Pay lots, come before 4PM to get a space
THOMAS GUIDE: 593 D4
KID-FRIENDLY * WHEELCHAIR/STROLLER ACCESS

Kwanzaa Gwaride Festival

LEIMERT PARK VILLAGE
Crenshaw Blvd & 43rd St, LA 90008
323-296-1532
www.kwanzaapeopleofcolor.homestead.com

Celebrate Kwanzaa, the seven-day African American New Year observance at the largest such event in the US. The Kwanzaa holiday is based on African "first fruits" celebrations and was established to continue the African principles of community. Kwanzaa begins the day after Christmas (Dec 25) and ends on the traditional New Year's Day (Jan 1). Activities are planned for each of the seven spiritual days of Kwanzaa including a community candle lighting ceremony for that day's principle. The parade is usually held in the middle of the weeklong celebration. It begins at Adams and Crenshaw Blvds and travels south to Leimert Park at Vernon Ave.

WHEN: Dec 26 to Jan 1
PARKING: Varies * **THOMAS GUIDE:** 673 E3
KID-FRIENDLY * **WHEELCHAIR/STROLLER ACCESS**

LA County Holiday Celebration

MUSIC CENTER, DOROTHY CHANDLER PAVILION
135 N Grand Ave, LA 90012
213-972-3099
www.lacountyarts.org

Looking for FREE spirited holiday entertainment the night before Christmas? Savvy Angelenos head for the six-hour musical performance marathon at the Dorothy Chandler Pavilion. Sponsored by the LA County Arts Commission, this FREE holiday gift has returned every Christmas Eve since 1964. Each year there are new and familiar artists—1,000 to 1,500 of them—from LA's diverse cultural population. Choirs, gospel singers and dance troupes perform everything from traditional carols to ethnic drama. Hear and see the jazz-rhythm tap version of "Deck the Halls," watch an excerpt of the traditional Nutcracker ballet and watch a young Mexican folkloric group create a *Las Posadas* procession on stage. No reservations required and seating is on a first come first seated basis. Doors open at 2:30PM. Stay for one performance or sit for all six hours. If you can't be there in person, local PBS station KCET runs the entire program live.

WHEN: 3PM to 9PM Dec 24
PARKING: FREE under Music Center ★ **THOMAS GUIDE:** 634 F3
KID-FRIENDLY ★ **WHEELCHAIR/STROLLER ACCESS**

LA Harbor Holiday Afloat Parade

PORTS O'CALL VILLAGE
1100 Nagoya Way, San Pedro 90731
310-832-7272 (chamber)
www.sanpedrochamber.com

Light up another child's Christmas while watching local mariner associations light up the LA Harbor. For 40+ years harbor-area service organizations and folks involved in the maritime industry and recreational boating having been floating a winter-lit procession on the water and using the parade participation fees to help local youth organizations. At the same time, the parade promoters sponsor a toy drive for kids. The luminous parade sails out of the Port of Los Angeles' East Basin and can be viewed for FREE from several locations: East Basin yacht marinas, Banning's Landing Community Center, SS Lane Victory in San Pedro, LA Maritime Museum and Ports O'Call Village. It takes about an hour for the parade to pass any one of these locations.

WHEN: 6PM Sat in Dec, date varies
PARKING: FREE (at Ports O'Call) ★ **THOMAS GUIDE:** 824 C6
KID-FRIENDLY ★ **WHEELCHAIR/STROLLER ACCESS**

LA Kings Downtown on Ice

PERSHING SQUARE
532 S Olive St, LA 90013
213-847-4970
www.laparks.org

It's an ice skating rink fit for a City of Angels and Kings and the 50' by 90' seasonal attraction glimmers in the glow of LA's skyscrapers. Sponsored by the LA Kings hockey team, the rink hosts several FREE events including youth hockey clinics, concerts, a snow day, a holiday festival and a live preview performance of "Disney on Ice." FREE one-hour hockey clinics for ages 7-14 and ages 15-adult include FREE use of hockey skates and equipment. FREE concerts during Tuesday and Thursday lunch hours and Friday nights. Public ice-skating does cost but not much— $6 per hour and $2 skate rental. Rink opens before Thanksgiving and continues after New Year's.

WHEN: Times vary so call or check Web site; open late Nov to early Jan
PARKING: Underground, $4 all day * **THOMAS GUIDE:** 634 F4
KID-FRIENDLY

Las Posadas

EL PUEBLO DE LOS ANGELES HISTORICAL MONUMENT
125 Paseo de la Plaza (Olvera Street), LA 90012
213-625-5045
www.olvera-street.com

Journey with a Mexican tradition and watch as the biblical Mary and Joseph's nine-day trek to Bethlehem is re-enacted in LA's historic plaza. The candlelight procession starts each night from Dec 16 to Dec 24 and lasts from about 7:15PM to 8PM. Dressed in traditional Mexican costumes with their faces aglow with candlelight, the processioners provide a mystical quality to the evening. Free live musical and dance entertainment before and after the procession, including *piñata* breaking for children. The Olvera Street merchants provide FREE *champurado* (special Mexican drink), *pan dulce* (sweet bread), hot punch and candy to visitors.

WHEN: 6PM to 10PM Dec 16 – Dec 23, 5PM to 9PM Dec 24
PARKING: Pay lots, metered street * **THOMAS GUIDE:** 634 G3
KID-FRIENDLY * **HISTORIC** * **WHEELCHAIR/STROLLER ACCESS**

Marina del Rey Holiday Boat Parade

BURTON CHACE PARK
13560 Mindinao Way, Marina del Rey 90292
310-670-7130
www.mdrboatparade.org

Festooned with thousands of lights, a flotilla of 70+ decorated boats sets sail in the main channel. Five minutes of sparkling fireworks light the way for the parade. Boat owners compete for prizes while landlubbers watch the spectacular sight. Look for tall ships, small yachts and sailboats, many with elaborate displays. Best viewing spots are Burton Chace Park and Fisherman's Village on Fiji Way.

WHEN: Sat eve in Dec, date varies
PARKING: Public lots, minimal fee * **THOMAS GUIDE:** 672 B7
KID-FRIENDLY

New Year's Day Swim

CABRILLO BEACH BATHHOUSE
3800 Stephen White Dr, San Pedro 90731
888-LA-PARKS or 213-473-7070
www.laparks.org

Take the plunge and join the Cabrillo Beach Polar Bears in their annual first day of the New Year swim. The water is guaranteed to be an icy temperature but it's refreshing for those who shed their winter wear to reveal their beach togs. You don't have to take a full swim to be an honorary "polar bear"—a little dip will do. FREE certificates to all participants. The event includes a visit to the recently restored 1932 Cabrillo Bathhouse, plus hot chocolate or coffee. Stay and watch the New Year's Day college football games but it costs $10 per person.

WHEN: Noon Jan 1
PARKING: $7 per car at Cabrillo Beach ∗ **THOMAS GUIDE:** 854 C2
KID-FRIENDLY

Open House at Rancho Los Cerritos

RANCHO LOS CERRITOS
4600 Virginia Rd, Long Beach 90807
562-570-1755
www.rancholoscerritos.org

Experience Christmas as it was in the 1870s at the oldest house in Long Beach. Built in 1844 by cattle rancher John Temple, the two-story Monterey style adobe later became the home of the pioneering Bixby family who lived and worked on the rancho. The Bixbys raised 30,000 sheep on the 27,000-acre property from the 1860s to 1880s. On one December Sunday afternoon, the historic 4.7-acre museum site holds a FREE holiday open house. Take a self-guided tour of the adobe, view the vintage Christmas ornaments, listen to live music and snack on light refreshments. Earlier in the month the rancho holds special candlelight re-enactments of the real life adventures of the Bixby family as they might have on Dec. 23, 1878. Dozens of living history actors portray 19th century family members and rancho workers. Tickets are only $6 each but should be purchased weeks in advance.

WHEN: (Open House) 1PM to 4PM, 2nd Sun in Dec, date varies
PARKING: FREE * **THOMAS GUIDE:** 765 D5
KID-FRIENDLY * **HISTORIC** * **WHEELCHAIR/STROLLER ACCESS**

Queen Mary Tree Lighting Ceremony

QUEEN MARY

1126 Queens Highway, Long Beach 90802

562-435-3511

www.queenmary.com

Step aboard the "Grey Ghost" and witness the annual lighting of the Christmas tree on this famous ocean liner turned entertainment complex. For a decade the Queen Mary has been creating holiday glow and inviting the public to see it for FREE. Normally it costs big bucks to spend time on this stunning ship permanently anchored in Long Beach harbor. Come early to the mid-week lighting event on the Sun Deck Stage at the ship's stern; FREE admission begins at 4:30PM. Listen to the International Children's Choir of Long Beach and snack on FREE refreshments from 6PM to 7PM. The lights are switched on at 7PM. Be sure to check out the elaborate Gingerbread holiday scene created by the Queen's pastry chef and on display in the Main Hall on the Promenade Deck.

WHEN: Weekday eve in early Dec
PARKING: $8 for 1 to 12 hours, parking reduced with validation
THOMAS GUIDE: 825 D3
KID-FRIENDLY * **WHEELCHAIR/STROLLER ACCESS**

Southern California Christmas

HOMESTEAD MUSEUM
15415 East Don Julian Rd, City of Industry 91745
626-968-8492
www.homesteadmuseum.org

Relive a Southern California Christmas from the 1840s, 1870s and 1920s when you reach back in time and spend a day at this historic homestead. The staff and volunteers for the six-acre historic site set up an afternoon holiday fair with FREE tours of its 1870s Workman House constructed around an 1840s adobe and the La Casa Nueva, a 1920s Spanish Colonial Revival mansion. Visit with living history characters on the tours and look for holiday decorations that match the time period. Listen to the sounds of a Victorian brass ensemble, watch performances of Las Posadas and join in with Christmas carolers. The historic museum hosts several children's activities such as stringing popcorn for tree garlands and visits with Santa Claus. Sample holiday treats and buy special gifts at the museum store. The museum also holds FREE guided tours highlighting the history of Christmas in California (1PM to 4PM Wed – Sun) throughout the holiday season.

WHEN: (Holiday Fair) 1PM to 5PM Sun in Dec, date varies (Holiday Tours) 1PM to 4PM Wed – Sun Dec 1 to Dec 30 (Closed Dec 24 – 25, Dec 31 – Jan 1)
PARKING: FREE * **THOMAS GUIDE:** 678 C1
KID-FRIENDLY * **HISTORIC** * **WHEELCHAIR/STROLLER ACCESS**

The Balian House

1960 Mendocino Lane, Altadena 91001
626-795-9311 (Pasadena Visitors & Convention Bureau)
www.pasadenacal.com

This Italian Renaissance mansion glistens like a holiday palace with 10,000 twinkling lights. For nearly half a century, the Balian family (of Balian Ice Cream manufacturing) has made the annual light show its gift to the community. The light-decked mansion is most awe-inspiring from blocks away, but park the car and wander around the perimeter of the sprawling lot to check out the life-size displays, ranging from the whimsical (Santa, his reindeer and a red-nosed Rudolph) to the religious (nativity scenes and angels). The attraction has become so popular that tour buses deliver hundreds of visitors and vendors hawk light sticks and snacks.

WHEN: Mid-December through January 1
PARKING: FREE on street * **THOMAS GUIDE:** 536 C6
KID-FRIENDLY

Universal CityWalk Holiday Entertainment

UNIVERSAL CITY WALK

1000 Universal Center Dr, Universal City 91608
818-622-4455
www.citywalkhollywood.com

California's themed pedestrian promenade and entertainment complex creates a Hollywood style winter wonderland with thousands of glittering lights and giant holiday decorations. The landmark site provides FREE entertainment from snowfalls to live concerts and other holiday entertainment. While you're out shopping or just having a good time, look for FREE stuff to do from visiting with costumed characters or entertaining the kids with holiday craft sessions. Look for tie-ins to Universal holiday movies and an outdoor skating rink (fee applies).

WHEN: Day after Thanksgiving to early Jan
PARKING: $8 * **THOMAS GUIDE:** 563 C6
KID-FRIENDLY * **WHEELCHAIR/STROLLER ACCESS**

Victorian Christmas

BANNING RESIDENCE MUSEUM

401 East M St, Wilmington 90744

310-548-7777

www.banningmuseum.org

Step into a Christmas from the past—a really old-fash-ioned Christmas without the commercial byproducts—when you celebrate a Victorian era holiday at this historic museum. Discover how Southern California observed the special holiday during the 1800s when everything—from ornaments to cookies—were made by hand. Take a tour of the former residence of General Phineas Banning and marvel at the Family Living Room's Christmas tree embellished with homemade paper chains, birds nests made from real eggshells, cardboard cornucopias filled with candy and paper scrap ornaments adorned with beads and sequins. At the Stagecoach Barn kids craft their own ornaments in FREE workshops and take them home to hang on their own trees. Retreat to the Schoolhouse for readings of Victorian Christmas stories, relax on the patio with apple cider and cookies or take a FREE ride in a horse drawn buggy to the nearby historic Drum Barracks. Reservations not required.

WHEN: 11AM to 4PM Sat & Sun in Dec
PARKING: FREE * **THOMAS GUIDE:** 794 F5
KID-FRIENDLY * **HISTORIC** * **WHEELCHAIR/STROLLER ACCESS**

Winter Holiday Festival

PERSHING SQUARE

532 S Olive St, LA 90013

213-847-4970

www.laparks.org

The coolest place to be in LA during the holiday season is Downtown on Ice which hosts this three-day weekend event. Walk among strolling entertainers and enjoy the

FREE live music. Decorate a tree, play FREE virtual snow games and let the kids make & take crafts from noon until night. Special entertainment for teens Friday evening, family entertainment Saturday and skating showcase on Sunday.

WHEN: Fri – Sat in Dec, dates vary
PARKING: Underground, $4 all day * **THOMAS GUIDE:** 634 F4
KID-FRIENDLY

Winterlit Celebration

SANTA MONICA PLACE
395 Santa Monica Pl, Santa Monica 90401
310-394-5451
www.santamonicaplace.com

Stroll through Santa Monica's version of a winter wonderland as the Santa Monica Place shopping area is draped in holiday lights from 18-foot-tall Christmas trees to faux icebergs on the ground and icicles hanging from light posts. A celebrity kicks off the festivities the day after Thanksgiving by switching on the lights and snow falls courtesy of a snow machine. The weeks-long sparkling spectacular is studded with winter holiday events including a menorah lighting, carolers, costumed characters, FREE gift wrapping days, crafts for kids and toy drives. Sip FREE cider at a open house, watch FREE outdoor holiday movies and bring your pet for a visit with a surfin' Santa Claus.

WHEN: Day after Thanksgiving through early Jan
PARKING: Three hours FREE in the two adjacent parking structures during shopping hours except after 5PM Thu - Sun. On those evenings, there is a $3 parking fee.
THOMAS GUIDE: 671 E2
KID-FRIENDLY * **WHEELCHAIR/STROLLER ACCESS**

Extra Events

CONCERTS

Concerts in the Park

CHUMASH PARK
5550 Medea Valley Dr, Agoura Hills 91301
818-597-7361
www.ci.agoura-hills.ca.us/recreation

Rock, swing, or just chill out to live music as the summer sun sets over a tranquil corner of the Conejo Valley. The City of Agoura Hills Parks and Recreation Department presents five Sunday evening concerts starting in late June in Chumash Park. Shows feature a wide variety of musical styles from oldies to modern rock to jazz. Past performers have included rock veterans the Marshall Tucker band and Al Stewart and jazz luminaries Pancho Sanchez and Jack Sheldon. Bring a blanket and a picnic dinner or score some munchies from the local food vendors on site. Come early as there is no reserved seating. No pets please.

WHEN: Summer, 6PM Sun eves
PARKING: FREE on street * **THOMAS GUIDE:** 558 B5
KID-FRIENDLY

Concerts in the Park

WARNER PARK

5800 Topanga Canyon Blvd, Woodland Hills 91364
818-704-1358
www.valleycultural.org

Cool off from the summer heat in the shade of dozens of tall trees while you soak in some live pop, classical, folk, and world music. Concerts at Warner Park in Woodland Hills are held Sunday at 6PM from June through August. Bring a lawn chair, a blanket, and a picnic dinner, or visit the on-site food court from 5PM to 7PM and choose from Japanese, Italian, Hawaiian, barbeque, and other cuisines. A West Valley cultural institution for over 25 years, this concert series is sponsored by the Valley Cultural Center, a nonprofit organization dedicated to the advancement of the arts in the San Fernando Valley.

WHEN: June through Aug, 6PM Sun eves
PARKING: FREE limited street, nearby pay structures ($3-$4)
THOMAS GUIDE: 560 A1
KID-FRIENDLY ★ WHEELCHAIR/STROLLER ACCESS

Jazz at LACMA

LA COUNTY MUSEUM OF ART

5905 Wilshire Blvd, LA 90036
323-857-6000
www.lacma.org

Blow off your end-of-week rush hour Westside commute and settle into jazz grooves on an outdoor pavilion at one of the country's premier cultural landmarks. Classical jazz dominates the scene at the LA County Museum of Art's Times Mirror Court Fridays from 5:30-8:30PM. Ample standing room is available on the plaza, but to get one of the 250 seats, arrive no later than 5PM. Two restaurants and a bar are adjacent to the pavilion. Heat lamps warm concert-goers in cooler months.

WHEN: Friday nights
PARKING: Pay lots ($4-5), metered street * **THOMAS GUIDE:** 633 B2

Marina del Rey Summer Concerts

BURTON CHACE PARK

13650 Mindinao Way, Marina del Rey 90292

310-305-9545

www.visitthemarina.com

Serenade yourself to the perfect Southern California sunset over the Pacific Ocean as you listen to the sounds of a symphonic or pops concert. The Marina del Rey Summer Symphony zings its strings on Thursday nights while pops singers from the likes of jazz artist Rene Marie to folk singer Judy Collins headline on Saturday evenings. Bring a picnic dinner and settle in on a blanket draped over the grass early. Concerts start at 7PM. Sponsored by Arrowhead Spring Water and the LA County Department of Beaches & Harbors.

WHEN: 7PM, Thu & Sat, July to Aug
PARKING: $2.00 LA County Lot # 4 on Mindanao Way, overflow parking in LA County Lot # 5 on Bali Way
THOMAS GUIDE: 672 B7
KID-FRIENDLY

Pershing Square Summer Concert Series

PERSHING SQUARE

532 S Olive St, LA 90013

888-LA-PARKS or 213-847-4970

www.laparks.org/pershingsquare/pershing.htm

Take a break from a stuffy office and relax in LA's oldest parks right in the middle of downtown. From here you can admire LA's surrounding architecture and enjoy the open-air park's renovated landscape with art installations all while listening to a lunchtime concert. Picnic on the grass or eat at the tables with umbrellas.

WHEN: June – Sept, Noon to 2PM, Tue & Thu, 3PM to 5PM
3rd Sun every month
PARKING: $4 under Pershing Square, all day;
pay lots & structures, prices vary; metered parking
THOMAS GUIDE: 634 E/F4
KID-FRIENDLY * **HISTORIC** * **WHEELCHAIR/STROLLER ACCESS**

Pershing Square Winter Concert Series

PERSHING SQUARE

532 S Olive St, LA 90013
213-847-4970
www.laparks.org/pershingsquare/pershing.htm

Take a break from work and squeezed-in holiday shopping and head for downtown's historic heart for the widest range of live music anywhere. You'll hear holiday music, of course, plus jazz, new age, country, blues, R & B, and zydeco. Tribute bands cover headliners such as Pat Benatar; Crosby, Stills, Nash & Young; Led Zeppelin and Tina Turner. These November to January concerts are from noon until 2PM midweek, 8PM to 10PM Fridays.

WHEN: Nov – Jan, Noon to 2PM mid-week; 8PM to 10PM Fri
PARKING: Pay lots and structures, prices vary
THOMAS GUIDE: 634 E/F4
KID-FRIENDLY * **WHEELCHAIR/STROLLER ACCESS**

Playboy Jazz in Brookside Park

OLD PASADENA SUMMER FEST

Brookside Park
360 N Arroyo Blvd, Pasadena 91105
626-797-6803
www.oldpasadenasummerfest.com

Zip over to the largest community event in the San Gabriel Valley and catch a daylong piece of the famous Playboy Jazz Festival for FREE. Held in conjunction with the Old Pasadena Summer Fest, the FREE concert offers the hottest performers in traditional and contemporary jazz, blues, R&B, Latin and Afro-Cuban music. Meet the performers afterwards in the Autograph Booth and have them sign a CD that you can buy on site. Held in Brookside Park just south of the Rose Bowl, the FREE concert is sponsored by the Playboy Jazz Festival, KTWV The Wave, KKJZ 88.1 FM and is supported in part by the Recording Industry Music Performance Trust Fund.

WHEN: Starting at 11AM daily, Memorial Weekend
PARKING: Adjacent to festival and pay public lots.
Avoid the 110 Pasadena Freeway that weekend
THOMAS GUIDE: 565 F4
KID-FRIENDLY * WHEELCHAIR/STROLLER ACCESS

Skirball Sunset Concert Series

SKIRBALL CULTURAL CENTER
2701 North Sepulveda Blvd, LA 90049
310-440-4500
www.skirball.org

Tour the world through the magic of music. The July and August courtyard concerts feature an eclectic blend of styles including uncommon fusions of Middle Eastern/electronica, Gypsy/klezmer, and Indian/jazz by musicians from diverse lands including Cuba, Zimbabwe, Nova Scotia, and Brazil. Doors open at 6:30PM; concerts begin at 7:30PM. Zeidler's Café offers a buffet dinner (reservations 310-440-4515). Museum is open and FREE until 10PM concert nights.

WHEN: July & Aug
PARKING: $5 * **THOMAS GUIDE:** 591 F9

Summer Concerts in the Park

CENTRAL PARK

27150 Bouquet Canyon Rd, Santa Clarita 91350
661-298-2787 or 661-286-4018
www.santa-clarita.com/arts/concerts

Let the music move your soul during Santa Clarita's Central Park summer concert series. An evening filled with stimulating tunes warms the heart, brightens the spirit and unites family, friends and even strangers. The series offers a variety of music to satisfy all tastes and preferences from jazz and blues to rock, country, disco and Latin rhythms. Last year's headliners included bands like Canned Heat and Boogie Nights.

WHEN: July & Aug, Sat eves
PARKING: Santa Clarita Transit sometimes offers special concert transportation arrangements. Contact the Cultural Affairs Office.
THOMAS GUIDE: 4461 A7
KID-FRIENDLY

Sunday Concert Series at the Santa Monica Pier

SANTA MONICA PIER

200 Santa Monica Blvd
Ocean and Colorado Aves, Santa Monica 90401
310-458-8901
www.santamonicapier.org

Spend Sunday on the famous Santa Monica Pier and hear an eclectic line-up of FREE music, weather permitting. Listen to zydeco, jazz, and classic oldies while strolling the pier's 1,000 feet of wooden boards and asphalt surface that jut out over the Pacific Ocean. The famous pier has been offering the FREE concerts for more than a decade. Consider taking a ride on the pier's 1922 antique carousel, listed in the National Registry of Historic Places. Rides are only 50 cents for kids and $1 for adults.

WHEN: 2PM to 4PM every Sun through Memorial Day (weather permitting)

PARKING: On the Pier Deck and the nearby beachfront. Limited short-term parking on metered streets. Max lot price is $6 Nov to Mar rising to $8 during the peak summer months.

THOMAS GUIDE: 671 E2

KID-FRIENDLY

Twilight Dance Series

SANTA MONICA PIER

200 Santa Monica Blvd
Ocean and Colorado Aves, Santa Monica 90401
310-458-8901
www.santamonicapier.org
310-458-8900

It may be the end of the line for the famed Route 66 but it's the beginning of a breezy series of summer dance concerts that attracts 10,000 people. The Twilight Dance Series spins its summer musical magic every Thursday night during the summer. Bop to the rhythms of a wide range of World Music from Latin jazz to a fusion of Celtic music and African instruments to modern techno pop. The mid-week concerts have been a happening on the pier for two decades.

WHEN: 7:30PM Thu June through Aug

PARKING: On the Pier Deck and nearby beachfront. Limited short-term parking on metered streets. Max lot price is $6 Nov to Mar rising to $8 during the peak summer months.

THOMAS GUIDE: 671 E2

KID-FRIENDLY * WHEELCHAIR/STROLLER ACCESS

Wild Wednesdays

TORRANCE CULTURAL ARTS CENTER

3330 Civic Center Dr, Torrance 90503

310-781-7150

www.torrancelive.us

Spend a wild Wednesday afternoon in the Torrance Cultural Arts Center's Torino Plaza. The diverse schedule of musical performers changes every summer. You might hear any genre from country to Celtic to swing. It's a nice way to spend your lunch hour or a tourist break. Bring your own or buy from one of the fresh food vendors on the site. Check the Web site for the latest line-up

WHEN: Noon Wed, mid-June to late Aug

PARKING: FREE * **THOMAS GUIDE:** 763 E5

KID-FRIENDLY * **WHEELCHAIR/STROLLER ACCESS**

World City

WALT DISNEY CONCERT HALL

W.M. Keck Foundation Children's Amphitheatre

135 N Grand Ave, LA 90012

213-972-7211

www.musiccenter.org

Move to the global rhythms of the FREE Saturday performances especially designed for the W.M. Keck Foundation Children's Amphitheatre at the stunning new Walt Disney Concert Hall. That's right, admission-FREE concerts at this 300-seat outdoor performance space. The series of six music, dance and theatre performances cater to families with children of all ages and are offered at various times throughout the year. The line-up always includes internationally renowned touring ensembles and professional artists. The performances feature world cultures from Korean classical dance to Eskimo songs. To top it off, World City events include pre- and post-performance family activities that tie in with the specific ethnic heritages represented. Activities such as art workshops and storytelling are held in the adjacent Blue Ribbon Garden. No tickets required; seating is on a first come, first seated basis.

WHEN: Select Sat afternoon, dates vary
PARKING: Steep; up to $17 max in Music Center garage
THOMAS GUIDE: 634 F3
KID-FRIENDLY ∗ **WHEELCHAIR/STROLLER ACCESS**

Captioned Film Series

PASADENA PUBLIC LIBRARY
DONALD R. WRIGHT AUDITORIUM
285 E Walnut St, Pasadena 91101

626-744-4066

www.ci.pasadena.ca.us/library/

Watch a FREE captioned classic feature film every Wednesday afternoon at the Pasadena Public Library. There's a different screening held in the Donald R. Wright Auditorium each week. While sitting in the popular auditorium's red plush seats watch old classics such as *Shane, Of Human Bondage* and *The Woman in Question.* You can find out the current month's movie titles by calling the library or any of Pasadena's branch libraries.

WHEN: 1PM to 3 PM Weds
PARKING: FREE for 3 hours in library lot off Garfield Ave
THOMAS GUIDE: 565 J4

CSUN Cinematheque

ELAINE AND ALAN ARMER THEATER
MANZANITA HALL,
CAL STATE UNIVERSITY NORTHRIDGE

18111 Nordhoff St, Northridge 91325

818-677-3943

www.CSUNcinematheque.com

Attend a film festival without the crowds, ticket hassles, or Westside traffic. Cal State Northridge's Department of Cinema and Television Arts holds year-round afternoon and evening screenings of first-run and classic films built around fascinating themes that appeal to film buffs and casual cinema fans alike. The programs are held at the campus's Elaine and Alan Armer Theater, a state-of-the-art, 125 seat venue. Some presentations are augmented by lectures from CSUN faculty members, authors, and actors as well as panel discussions with film experts. A complete schedule for the current year is on the Cinematheque's Web site.

WHEN: Several evening screenings each month, dates vary
PARKING: $4 on campus (exact change required)
THOMAS GUIDE: 501 A7
WHEELCHAIR/STROLLER ACCESS

Holiday Movie Shorts

SANTA MONICA PLACE

395 Santa Monica Pl, Santa Monica 90401

310-394-5451

www.santamonicaplace.com

If you need a quick film fix during your Tuesday night holiday shopping, stop by Santa Monica Place. A series of holiday movie shorts are double projected on the shopping center's upper parking deck every Tuesday in December. The deck is reserved for moviegoers only and the shorts give you're a break from choosing gifts. You can also view the movies from the Promenade but without the sound.

WHEN: Tue eve in Dec, date varies
PARKING: Three hours FREE in the two adjacent parking structures during shopping hours except after 5PM Thu - Sun.
On those evenings, there is a $3 parking fee.
THOMAS GUIDE: 671 E2
KID-FRIENDLY ★ **WHEELCHAIR/STROLLER ACCESS**

Melnitz Movies

UCLA CAMPUS
James Bridges Theatre (Melnitz 1409)
405 Hilgard Ave, LA 90095
310-825-4321
gsa.asucla.ucla.edu/~melnitz/

Sneak preview top winners from film festivals around the world, as well as first class documentaries, for FREE, courtesy of the UCLA Graduate Student Association. Offered to the UCLA community, including students, staff, faculty and guests, the movies may include Q & A sessions with directors, producers and actors. All the films are either official selections of or have won top honors from festivals such as Cannes, Sundance, Sedona and Toronto. Show times are usually 7:30PM Tuesday and Thursday nights with some exceptions. Check the Web site for a current schedule. FREE tickets are available the day of the screening at the Melnitz Box Office 30 minutes before show time.

WHEN: Ongoing, usually 7:30PM Tue or Thu
PARKING: $7 in UCLA lot, closest one is P3 off Sunset Blvd or Hilgard Ave
THOMAS GUIDE: 632 B2

Movies under the Stars

CALABASAS TENNIS AND SWIM CENTER (JULY)
23400 Park Sorrento, Calabasas 91302

JUAN BAUTISTA DEANZA PARK (AUGUST)
3701 Lost Hills Rd, Calabasas 91302
818-880-6461
www.cityofcalabasas.com

Tired of noisy, crowded indoor theaters? Hate paying nearly $10 for tickets to the newest flick? Then bring the kids and some lounge chairs or a blanket and enjoy a summer evening movie with the City of Calabasas picking up the tab. The city presents G or PG-rated movies on a huge screen at the Calabasas Tennis and Swim center in July and at DeAnza Park in August (one screening at each venue). Seating is on the lawn. Shows start at 8:30. Candy and soft drinks are available at the concession stand.

WHEN: 8:30PM July & Aug
PARKING: FREE lots
THOMAS GUIDE: 559 F4 (Tennis and Swim Center) and 588 G1 (DeAnza Park)
KID-FRIENDLY * **WHEELCHAIR/STROLLER ACCESS**

Outdoor Picture Show

MEDIA CITY CENTER
IKEA Courtyard (I-5 at Burbank Blvd), Burbank 91502
818-566-8617
www.mediacitycenter.com

Remember old-fashioned drive-in movies? Burbank's brought them back—but without the car—and without the cost! Every Wednesday at 7:00PM from late June-mid-August, the Media City Center turns the IKEA Courtyard into a giant outdoor theater complete with bleachers and a 20' by 16' screen. As the sun sets, you'll be entertained by musicians, face painters, balloon artists, and magicians. Visit the food court and sample specialties from nearby restaurants. Then at 8:30PM, sit back and watch a family-friendly movie under the stars. A drive-in style concession stand has candy, popcorn, and other movie munchies with the proceeds going to Burbank community service groups. Check the Web site for this summer's schedule.

WHEN: 7PM Weds, late June – mid-Aug
PARKING: FREE lot, structure, and street parking
THOMAS GUIDE: 533 G6
KID-FRIENDLY ★ WHEELCHAIR/STROLLER ACCESS

Rudolph Valentino Tribute

HOLLYWOOD FOREVER CEMETERY
6000 Santa Monica Blvd, Hollywood 90038
323-469-1181
www.forevernetwork.com

Rudy! Rudy! Rudy! In the early Twenties, that was the anguished cry from swooning women the world over when the dark, flickering image of dashing Rudolph Valentino, Hollywood's original Latin lover, shimmered across the silver screen. Born Rodolpho Alfonzo Rafaelo Pierre Filibert Guglielmi di Valentina d'Antonguolla, the Great Lover's meteoric rise from humble Italian immigrant to film immortal in exotic romantic films like *The Sheik* (1921) was cut short at the pinnacle of his career by his untimely death from complications of appendicitis in 1926. Eight decades later, on the Saturday after the anniversary of Valentino's death (Aug 23), Hollywood Forever Cemetery keeps his spirit aflame with it's annual FREE silent film tribute, held in front of the actual cathedral mausoleum where the immortal Lover found his eternal rest. Bring a picnic, spread your blanket under the stars, and discover the erotic charms of the Dark Lover, complete with live musical accompaniment by nonagenarian silent picture organist Bob Mitchell.

WHEN: 1st Sat eve on or after Aug 23
PARKING: FREE * **THOMAS GUIDE:** 593 G6
KID-FRIENDLY

Universal CityWalk's Summer "Drive-In" Movie Series

1000 Universal Center Dr, Universal City 91608
818-622-4455
www.citywalkhollywood.com

Drive-in to the movies a la Fred Flintstone—using your feet —and experience classic movies under the stars on CityWalk's giant outdoor 18' by 22' Astrovision Screen. Every summer, from early June to late August, CityWalk screens top-run films every Tuesday and Thursday night at 8PM. The Sci-Fi Channel sponsors Tuesday night's line-up with blockbusters such as "Star Wars," "The Matrix" and "Spider-Man." Thursdays are reserved for a collection of contemporary classics such as "Shrek," "Harry Potter and the Sorcerer's Stone" and "The Princess Bride." Park your car in the CityWalk lot and bring your picnic blanket and beach chairs for "front row" seating. No clunky boxes to fool with to hear the movies—the films are broadcast in virtual surround sound. Stock up on snacks or order a meal from a CityWalk take-out place and dine al fresco while enjoying the FREE show. Visit the Web site for a complete schedule.

WHEN: 8PM Tue & Thu, early June to late Aug
PARKING: $8 * **THOMAS GUIDE:** 563 C6
KID-FRIENDLY * **WHEELCHAIR/STROLLER ACCESS**

GARDENING GOODIES

Community Compost

RANCHO LAS VIRGENES COMPOSTING FACILITY

3700 Las Virgenes Rd, Calabasas 91302

818-251-2200

www.lvmwd.dst.ca.us/comm

Grab a bag, bucket, or barrel and fill 'em with FREE gourmet vittles for your garden. Every Saturday morning, the Las Virgenes Metropolitan Water District in Calabasas opens its plant to the community and gives away compost produced during its wastewater reclamation process. The district provides shovels as well as masks to prevent dust inhalation. Information about uses and content of the compost is available on the district's Web site.

WHEN: Sat mornings
PARKING: FREE ★ **THOMAS GUIDE:** 588 H1

Cool Trees Program

PASADENA WATER & POWER
Answerline: 626-744-6970
www.pwpweb.com

Shade your house and cut down on air conditioning costs by planting a leafy tree. Pasadena Water & Power provides FREE tree-planting workshops where you get advice on which tree to choose, information on tree care and expert planting tips. Attendees receive FREE tree stakes, mulch, arbor guards and more. Plus, PWP customers get a $40 rebate on each tree ($200 max) purchased within the Pasadena city limits. Rebate is $30 per tree ($150 max) for trees bought outside city limits. Call the PWP Answerline or visit the Web site for workshop dates and times.

WHEN: Year round

Free Mulch and Firewood

WHITTIER FERTILIZER
9441 Kruse Rd, Whittier 90660
562-801-2489 ext. 3522 (City Environmental Coordinator/
Any Time Line)
www.ci.pico-rivera.ca.us/community/freemulch.html

Live in Pico Rivera? The city provides its residents with FREE mulch and firewood every third Saturday during certain months (check the city calendar each year). Provide proof of residency, bring your own container and you can shovel up to 33 gallons of the soil enriching material. Additional mulch costs only a buck per 33 gallons. Firewood is also available while supplies last.

WHEN: 8AM to 3PM, daily
PARKING: FREE * **THOMAS GUIDE:** 676 J1

Gardening Hotline

UNIVERSITY OF CALIFORNIA COOPERATIVE EXTENSION

323-260-3238

www.ucanr.org

E-mail mglosangeleshelpline@ucdavis.edu

Stumped by a gardening problem? Find a solution by tapping into the University of California Cooperative Extension's FREE Common Ground Garden Program helpline for LA gardeners. Leave a detailed query with your name, mailing address and phone number and a Master Gardener will contact you.

Got Mulch?

LA CITY DEPARTMENT OF PUBLIC WORKS

818-834-5128

www.ci.la.ca.us/DPW/dpwhome.htm

What can help your garden grow? Mulch, a layer of dead plant matter and clippings, that keeps moisture in and promotes proper soil drainage. There's nothing better for your prized roses or vegetable garden than organically cured mulch. And you can get it FREE from the LA City Department of Public Works/Bureau of Sanitation at four locations. Made from clean yard clippings and de-weeded, the mulch is prepared in San Pedro. Bring your own shovel, bag or pick-up truck and dig in! Availability is subject to change.

REFUSE COLLECTION YARD
1400 N Gaffey St, San Pedro 90731
WHEN: 7AM to 5PM daily
PARKING: FREE * THOMAS GUIDE: 824 B2

LOPEZ CANYON LANDFILL
11950 Lopez Canyon Rd @ Paxton St, Lake View Terrace 91342
WHEN: 7AM to dusk, daily
PARKING: FREE * THOMAS GUIDE: 482 H3

NORTHRIDGE METROLINE STATION
Open lot on Wilbur Ave north of Parthenia St, Northridge 91324
WHEN: Daylight hours; most popular site; mulch delivered Mon, Wed, Fri
PARKING: FREE * **THOMAS GUIDE:** 530 H1

BULKY ITEM PICKUP YARD
2649 E Washington Blvd, East LA 90058
North side of Washington, just west of the LA River
WHEN: 9AM to 5PM, daily; closed holidays
PARKING: FREE * **THOMAS GUIDE:** 674 J1

Pageant of the Roses Free Pruning Workshop

ROSE HILLS MEMORIAL PARK

3888 S Workman Mill Rd, Whittier 90601
562-699-0921
www.rosehills.com

Prune those prickly rose bushes properly after attending this FREE annual pruning demonstration held in one of Southern California's most vibrant rose gardens—the Pageant of Roses Garden at Rose Hills Memorial Park, the world's largest single-operated cemetery. Held at the beginning of the New Year, the workshop includes a demonstration and lecture by Dr. Tommy Cairns, curator of the gardens and president of The World Federation of the Rose Society. Then take our your shears and test your skills with the help of the garden staff who also hold a question and answer session.

WHEN: Early January
PARKING: FREE * **THOMAS GUIDE:** 677 C1

Smart Gardening Workshops

LA COUNTY DEPARTMENT OF PUBLIC WORKS
888-CLEAN LA
www.smartgardening.com

Discover how to use less water, recycle yard waste and create a beautiful and bountiful garden with the techniques taught at these FREE LA County Department of Public Works seminars. Learn how to use lawn trimmings, recycle kitchen scraps and establish a worm-composting bin at one of 12 Smart Gardening Learning Centers throughout the county. Click on the Web site's workshops & schedules link or call the number for a schedule. Each center's demonstration areas are open during the workshops. No reservations required.

WHEN: Weekends, dates vary
PARKING: Varies * **THOMAS GUIDE:** Varies

Trees for a Green LA

LA DEPARTMENT OF WATER & POWER
800-GreenLA
www.ladwp.com

Give your house, your yard, your neighborhood some FREE shade. Sponsored by the LA Department of Water and Power, this Earth-friendly program lets city residents receive up to seven FREE shade trees selected from 40 different species. To participate you must attend a workshop that teaches how to plan for, plant and protect the young trees. With the help of the LA Conservation Corps and other non-profit organizations, several citywide workshops are offered each month. A trained neighborhood forester guides you in drafting a planting plan specific to your needs and location. The FREE trees are delivered about two weeks later, for FREE. So far, more than 10,000 shade trees have been planted through this program.

WHEN: Monthly
PARKING: Varies * **THOMAS GUIDE:** Varies

Wildflower Hotline

THEODORE PAYNE FOUNDATION
10459 Tuxford St, Sun Valley 91352
818-768-3533 (Wildflower Hotline)
818-768-1802 (Foundation)
www.theodorepayne.org

Blowing along with the winds in March are seeds from Southern California's native wildflowers that sprout riotously when there have been good rains in February. To find out where the signature orange California poppies and the blue dove lupines are popping up, call the Theodore Payne Foundation's FREE Wildflower Hotline: 818-768-3533. Dedicated to preserving and propagating native California plants, the foundation keeps tabs on 40 different wildflower sites. Discover where these blankets of color are blooming, then take a drive for a FREE floral show. New wildflower sightings are also listed on the Web site.

WHEN: Early Mar through May

ONGOING EVENTS

Clockers' Corner at Santa Anita Park

SANTA ANITA PARK
285 W Huntington Dr, Arcadia 91007
626-574-7223
www.santaanita.com

The Marx Brothers cavorted through this 70-year-old race-track in *A Day at the Races*. Nowadays, take a slower pace with the family and head over to Clockers' Corner, located at the west end of the track. Reasonably priced Continental breakfasts are served here, but since you're not spending any money head over to the grandstands. Watch thorough-breds run through their early-morning workouts with the San Gabriel Mountains as a backdrop.

WHEN: 7:30AM to 10AM, daily, Dec 26 to late Apr
PARKING: FREE * **THOMAS GUIDE:** 567 C6
KID-FRIENDLY

Home Depot How-to Clinics

HOME DEPOT
Various Locations
800-430-3376
www.homedepot.com

Looking to fix up your home for FREE? Well, you may not get the supplies for FREE but you can get FREE labor when you do it yourself. Home Depot makes it easy with its FREE How-to clinics that provide homeowners with the know-how to install ceramic tile, create a faux painting effect on walls and put in a new parquet floor. Most of the hands-on classes are held during weekday evenings and late morning/early afternoon on Saturdays and Sundays. Clinics last for one hour and Home Depot experts offer step-by-step instructions for each project. There are more than 35 Home Depot stores in the LA area, so a FREE clinic isn't hard to find.

WHEN: Weekday eves, late morning/early afternoon Sat & Sun
PARKING: FREE * **THOMAS GUIDE:** Varies

Home Depot Kids Workshops

HOME DEPOT
Various Locations
800-430-3376
www.homedepot.com

Let professionals teach your kids basic carpentry and gardening skills at Home Depot's FREE kids workshops for ages 6 to 12. Kids can build a birdhouse, a model train, a letter holder, or a child-sized toolbox. Home Depot associates patiently show children how to piece together each project, glue and paint. Gardening experts also offer workshops where kids pot plants and grow seedlings. Children not only learn how to be patient themselves and to follow directions, but to clean up after a project and to return all borrowed tools. Children are given a certificate of accomplishment along with their finished project. Kids workshops are held the first Saturday of every month at all of the 35 Home Depot stores in the LA area.

WHEN: 9AM first Sat of every month
PARKING: FREE * **THOMAS GUIDE:** Varies
KID-FRIENDLY

Los Feliz First Friday Art Walk

Hollywood & Sunset Blvds, Los Feliz 90027
323-662-3279
www.ceart.com/artwalk

Gather with the artists whose work is showcased in the Los Feliz area's galleries every Friday night from 7PM to 11PM. Clustered in or near the triangle made where Hollywood Blvd meets Sunset Blvd, are a handful of galleries and studios who use the Art Walk night for their opening night receptions. Nurtured by Bert W. Green and his fine arts Circle Elephant Art Gallery, Art Walk's map can be downloaded from the gallery's Web site (www.ceart.com). One of the more notorious galleries along the walk is La Luz de Jesus, which presents "lowbrow art" consisting of post-pop paintings and sculptures. A more traditional art venue is the LA Municipal Art Gallery at Barnsdall Park, which starts and ends the walk early (5PM to 9PM). Where Santa Monica & Sunset Blvd meet is Gallery 4016, which shows giant art installations in its warehouse style space, and Arts & Books which offers art books and modern first editions along with exhibits of emerging California and international artists.

WHEN: 7PM to 11PM 1st Fri eve every month
PARKING: Metered street, pay lots * **THOMAS GUIDE:** 594 A4

MOCA's First Sundays are for Families

MUSEUM OF CONTEMPORARY ART

250 South Grand Avenue, LA 90012

213-621-1712

www.moca.org

Give your kids a fun museum experience as they learn about contemporary art and then make their own. Artist-educators give short museum tours that highlight an artist or particular field of modern art before leading youngsters ages 7-18 in workshops where they create sculptures, paintings, monuments or other works of art. Tours and instruction are offered in English and Spanish; other languages are available upon request.

WHEN: 1st Sun every month
PARKING: FREE lot * **THOMAS GUIDE:** 634 F3
KID-FRIENDLY

Montrose Art Walk

2300 and 2400 blocks of Honolulu Ave, Montrose 91020

818-249-7171

www.montrosechamber.org/artwalk.html

Appreciate art and artists in their natural habitat four Saturdays this year. Painters, sculptors, ceramic creators and other fine artists from Montrose and surrounding communities exhibit at this homey but hip downtown area. FREE demonstrations of their technique and talent. Stroll the avenue, have a coffee at a sidewalk café, and imagine you're at Montmartre. Perhaps you'll even fall in love with a masterpiece.

WHEN: Four Sats throughout the year
PARKING: FREE * **THOMAS GUIDE:** 534 G3

Mt. Wilson Observatory Tours

SKYLINE PARK

Red Box Road, Angeles National Forest

310-476-4413

www.mwoa.org/tour.html

On a clear day you can see the antenna-strewn peak of Mt. Wilson. Why not drive up there one weekend and check out the observatory's collection of astronomical telescopes? From April through October (weather permitting), docents take you on a FREE tour of the astronomical museum, UCLA's 150-foot solar tower telescope and the 100-inch Hooker telescope, the world's largest until 1948 when a 200-incher was built atop Mt. Palomar. Just show up at the pavilion area, a few steps from the spacious parking lot, at 1PM on Saturday or Sunday. Bring your jacket. At 5700 feet, Mt. Wilson can be chilly. Visit on your own, weekdays, 10AM to 4PM. Self-guided tour brochures are FREE at the museum or through the observatory Web site. Take the 210 Freeway and exit at Angeles Crest Highway; drive north towards the mountains for about 14 miles. When you see the "Mount Wilson" sign, turn right and follow the road another 5 miles to the top. Keep your headlights on while driving; otherwise you may have to pay a hefty fine.

WHEN: 1PM Sat & Sun, Apr to Oct

PARKING: You must purchase a "Forest Adventure Pass" for $5 sold through sporting goods stores. Also available on weekends at the Clear Creek Ranger Station half way up the road to Mt. Wilson.

THOMAS GUIDE: 506 J7

KID-FRIENDLY

Musical Circus

PASADENA CIVIC AUDITORIUM

300 E Green St, Pasadena 91101

626-793-7172 Ext 10

www.pasadenasymphony.org

Broaden your family's musical horizons at Pasadena Symphony's musical instrument "petting zoo." Young musicians demonstrate the workings of orchestral instruments, then invite the under-10 set to pluck strings, fiddle with the percussion, or blast a few horns. Afterwards enjoy FREE interactive family-oriented concerts ranging from the Pasadena Youth Symphony to an All-American Sing Along.

WHEN: 8:30AM to 10AM, monthly, Oct to May
PARKING: Fee for public lots, metered streets * **THOMAS GUIDE:** 565 J5
KID-FRIENDLY

Pit 91 Annual Excavation

HANCOCK PARK
PAGE MUSEUM OF LA BREA DISCOVERIES

5801 Wilshire Blvd, LA 90036

323-934-PAGE

www.tarpits.org

When it's hot, tar oozing beneath Hancock Park really starts to bubble up to the surface. Walk through the park in summer and you'll see it coming through the grass, the sidewalk and spurting up like geysers in the lake. Hancock Park's La Brea Tar Pits is proof that LA experienced a prehistoric time when saber-toothed cats and tusked mammoths roamed the region. Not only is the tar active but so are the scientists in Pit 91, the Tar Pits biggest fossil excavation site. The Page Museum, operated by the Museum of Natural History of LA County, offers a FREE observation area. Look into the deep pit and watch paleontologists and volunteers dig into the sticky substance, which is really asphalt. All summer long they pry out preserved dire wolves teeth, giant sloth skulls and ancient bison bones. While the observation deck is FREE, there is an admission charge to the museum, except on the first Tuesday of each month when admission is FREE.

WHEN: 10AM to 4PM Wed – Sun, late June to early Sept
PARKING: $6 in Page Museum lot with museum validation, $8 without museum validation, metered street
THOMAS GUIDE: 633 C2
KID-FRIENDLY ∗ **WHEELCHAIR/STROLLER ACCESS**

Pomona Art Walk

POMONA ARTS COLONY
Downtown Pomona
Second Street at Garey Ave, Pomona 91766
909-868-2970
www.pomonaartcolony.com

Be a part of Downtown Pomona's Renaissance from a blighted blip on the map to a hip cultural hangout. Located on the east end of LA County's border, Pomona is attracting a new community of residents hungry for culture. Its downtown is now home to its own artists colony of 12+ galleries and studios. Located west of Garey Avenue, the galleries are mostly on or near downtown's Second Street. Look for the metal archway announcing the colony. So bustling is the art scene here that a charter high school devoted to the arts recently opened right in the heart of the colony. Simultaneous opening receptions are held at the galleries, which range from a glassworks showcase to the Cuttress Gallery, which exhibits new and emerging artists. Live entertainment from street performers to musicians happens at the Thomas Street Plaza where you'll also find the Southern California Artists organization's gallery in the Founders Building.

WHEN: 6PM to 9PM, 2nd Sat every month
PARKING: FREE ∗ **THOMAS GUIDE:** 640 J2
KID-FRIENDLY ∗ **WHEELCHAIR/STROLLER ACCESS**

Stories on Sundays

SKIRBALL CULTURAL CENTER
2701 N Sepulveda Blvd, LA 90049
310- 440-4500
www.skirball.org

Bring your kids (ages 3+) to the Skirball Cultural Center for stories that will stimulate their imagination and entertain them at the same time. Readings are based on monthly historical and cultural themes. Stories are told by literacy advocates from BookPALS, a volunteer organization of members of the Screen Actors Guild. Readings take place from 1:30PM – 2PM in the Kids Corner in the Resource center.

WHEN: 1:30PM to 2PM every Sun
PARKING: FREE * **THOMAS GUIDE:** 591 F1
KID-FRIENDLY * **WHEELCHAIR/STROLLER ACCESS**

The Getty Family Festival

THE GETTY
1200 Getty Center Dr, LA 90049
310-440-7300
www.getty.edu

Inspire to bring art into your family's life by actively participating in this daylong celebration where an era of art is brought to life through storytelling, dance, theater, and live music. Linked to a new Getty exhibition, the fest incorporates elements of a specific artful time be it the Renaissance, Ancient Greece or Medieval. Kids engage in an artful life at interactive workshops designed to incorporate the style of the time. Before hand, admire the ancient art, discover the art of furniture making, or simply explore the exhibits. All events and museum admission are FREE.

The festival is usually held one time a year in the spring or summer months.

WHEN: Sat in spring or summer, date varies
PARKING: $5 ∗ **THOMAS GUIDE:** 591 G7
KID-FRIENDLY ∗ **WHEELCHAIR/STROLLER ACCESS**

Thursday Night On The Square

PONCITLAN SQUARE

9th St East between Ave Q-9 and Ave Q-10, Palmdale 93550
661-267-5611
www.cityofpalmdale.org

Sometimes it's cool to be square, especially when attending Thursday Night On The Square, a fun-filled summer of activities arranged by the City of Palmdale. Shop at the outdoor farmers' market, which offers a fresh crop of fruits and vegetables or indulge your taste buds in a variety of prepared foods. Listen to musical entertainment provided by the highlighted band of the night, which specializes in either rhythm & blues, jazz, swing, hip hop, Latin rock, classic rock or country tunes. The weekly events feature activities such as a Star-spangled Baby Parade, a sports night, a magic show, a Canine Costume Party, a nature scavenger hunt and a luau. Pets not allowed, except for dogs on the night of the Canine Costume Party.

WHEN: 5:30PM to 8:30PM every Thu,
mid-June through the 1st week in Sept
PARKING: FREE ∗ **THOMAS GUIDE:** 4286 B1
KID-FRIENDLY

Tram Tours at Santa Anita Park

SANTA ANITA PARK

285 W Huntington Dr, Arcadia 91007

626-574-7223

www.santaanita.com

Climb aboard Santa Anita's tram for a look at a racetrack that the bookies rarely see. Tours, complete with live commentary, take groups through the track's stable area. Of particular interest is Barn 38 where legendary Seabiscuit was stabled from 1937 to 1940. The walking portion of the tour strolls through Paddock Gardens, blanketed with thousands of ornamental flowers. See the statue of Seabiscuit and his jockey, George Woolf and get a "never before permitted" look inside the jockeys' room. The man-made beauty of Santa Anita's art deco facade is also an eye-catcher. Stop by the gift shop and peruse intriguing horse racing paraphernalia. Tours run on weekend mornings during the park's racing season (Dec 26 to late April), departing the tram boarding area across from the receiving barn.

WHEN: 8AM, 9AM, 9:45AM, Sat & Sun, Dec 26 to late Apr
PARKING: FREE * **THOMAS GUIDE:** 567 C6
KID-FRIENDLY

Academy of Motion Picture Arts & Sciences Academy Gallery

8949 Wilshire Blvd, Beverly Hills 90211
310-247-3000
www.oscars.org

Get close to the golden boy statue, Oscar, at the institution responsible for awarding him to actors, actresses, producers, directors, screenwriters and other famous film folk. While you have to have the credentials to be part of the academy, you can visit its exhibition gallery. Located on the luxurious fourth floor, the grand gallery displays photos, posters and assorted movie artifacts, many not often seen elsewhere. Glance upstairs and you'll see a giant replica of Oscar himself, just outside the Academy theater entrance.

HOURS: 10AM to 5PM Tue – Fri, Noon to 6PM Sat & Sun, Closed Mon
PARKING: Pay lots, metered street ∗ **THOMAS GUIDE:** 632 H2

African-American Firefighter Museum

1401 S Central Ave, LA 90021
213-744-1730
www.lafd.org/aafm.htm

Discover how George W. Bright, the first black member of the LA Fire Department, rose through the ranks to become the first LAFD officer in 1902. His history and that of the first all Black and Latino fire brigade, live on in the century-old fire station that housed Engine Company 30 and Truck 11. Photographs, uniforms and firefighting equipment detail how Black firefighters battled blazes and sizzling segregation. Docents are available to answer questions about the cultural displays in this fire service museum, one of three in LA (all listed in this chapter) and 300 in the US.

HOURS: 10AM to 2PM Tue and Thu, 1PM to 4PM,
2nd and 4th Sun every month
PARKING: Street ★ **THOMAS GUIDE:** 634 F7
KID-FRIENDLY ★ **HISTORIC**

Bolton Hall Museum

10110 Commerce Ave, Tujunga 91042
818-352-3420
www.verdugo-online.com/clubs/boltonhall.htm

LA City Historical Monument number 2 is a prime architectural example of a boulder house and a desire to live off the land. Designed by "Nature Builder" George Harris in 1913, this building built with Tujunga Wash river rocks was a clubhouse for the "Little Landers," a society of Utopianists who settled the community of Tujunga. The house was named after author Bolton Hall, friend of Little Landers founder William E. Smythe. Eventually abandoned, the bold stone structure was rescued by the Little Landers Historical Society. Now the society's headquarters and library, the museum contains artifacts, photos and memorabilia of the Sunland-Tujunga area from the Gabrieleno Indians to the hall's renovation.

HOURS: 1PM to 4PM Sun - Tue
PARKING: FREE onsite * **THOMAS GUIDE:** 504 A4
HISTORIC

California African-American Museum

EXPOSITION PARK
600 State Dr, LA 90037
213-744-7432
www.caam.ca.gov

Visit the "keepers of the flame" of African American culture and history at this museum that chronicles and archives the African American journey of life. Designed by two African American architects, Jack Haywood and Vincent Proby, the building is tucked between two museum giants – the California Science Center and the Museum of Natural History. First opened during the 1984 Olympic Games, the recently renovated museum details the Black experience in the American West. It continues to diversify its collection of millions of artifacts—letters, manuscripts, photographs and garments—with film and music recordings in addition to sculptures and other art objects. One of only four state-operated museums, CAAM offers new exhibits, concerts and workshops throughout the year.

HOURS: 10AM to 4PM Wed - Sat
PARKING: $6 * **THOMAS GUIDE:** 674 B2
KID-FRIENDLY * **WHEELCHAIR/STROLLER ACCESS**

California Science Center

EXPOSITION PARK

700 State Dr, LA 90037
323-SCIENCE
www.casciencectr.org

Discover the secrets of science in this re-invention and expansion of the former Museum of Science & Industry. Redesigned and re-opened in 1998, the 245,000-square-foot science center continues to astound visitors with its wide range of interactive exhibits. Located on three levels, begin your scientific exploration before even entering the building. Outside, the center's Science Plaza contains art objects with scientific senses. Inside, Hypar, a five-story moving sculpture invented by Chuck Hoberman, greets you. Above you brave visitors pedal a bicycle on a high wire. On the upper levels discover technological advances in communications, transportation and structure in the Creative World gallery then delve into life's mysteries in the World of Life exhibit, where you'll meet Tess, a 50-foot human body simulator. On weekends, the science really heats up with FREE Science Spectacular shows, a slime bar where kids make their own squishy ooze and a 15-minute movie in the Cell Theater. There's also an Imax Theater, but that and the high wire bicycle and other simulators require paid tickets.

HOURS: 10AM to 5PM daily. Closed Thanksgiving,
Christmas & New Year's Day.
PARKING: $6 in center lot off 39th St * **THOMAS GUIDE:** 674 B2
KID-FRIENDLY * **WHEELCHAIR/STROLLER ACCESS**

California Science Center Air and Space Gallery

EXPOSITION PARK
700 State Dr, LA 90037
323-SCIENCE
www.casciencectr.org

Wing it to LA's premier aerospace museum. Located on the east end of the California Science Center's Exposition Park complex, the museum is a monument to flight, inside and out. Before you even enter its expansive interior with 75-foot ceiling, you'll see a fighter jet perched on the side of the Frank Gehry-built building. Inside are interactive exhibits designed to educate and entertain visitors about the science of flight in the air and in space. Suspended from the vaulted ceiling are real and replica aircraft from a F20 Northrop jet fighter (the only one still in existence) to a recently refurbished full-scale model of a 1902 Wright Glider. See an actual Gemini 11 capsule, flown by astronauts Pete Conrad and Dick Gordon and a Mercury-Redstone 2 capsule, which carried Ham, a chimpanzee, on a short flight.

HOURS: 10AM to 5PM daily. Closed Thanksgiving, Christmas & New Year's Day.
PARKING: $6 in center lot off 39th St * **THOMAS GUIDE:** 674 B2
KID-FRIENDLY * **WHEELCHAIR/STROLLER ACCESS**

Conservatory of Puppetry Arts

980 N Fairoaks Ave, Pasadena 91103
626-296-1536
www.copa-puppets.org

Puppets dance in the aisles at this museum featuring the 3,000-piece collection of puppeteer Alan Cook including Chinese rod puppets, Taiwanese hand puppets and American-made marionettes. Discover puppets carved from wood, sewn from embroidered cloth and crafted with porcelain heads. The only museum in Southern California to celebrate the magical art of puppetry, the facility recently moved into the American Friends Service Committee Headquarters. There are puppet projects for kids and a research library. The museum participates in the FREE Pasadena Art Night in March & October and offers FREE events throughout the year.

HOURS: 10AM to 4PM Mon - Tue and by appointment
PARKING: South side of building * **THOMAS GUIDE:** 565 H4
KID-FRIENDLY * **WHEELCHAIR/STROLLER ACCESSIBLE**

Discovery Lab

CABRILLO MARINE AQUARIUM

3720 Stephen White Dr, San Pedro 90731
310-548-7563
www.cabrilloaq.org

Kids use microscopes, observe live animals and explore sea specimens when they drop in at the Cabrillo Marine Aquarium's after-school discovery center. The Discovery Lab features a new hands-on activity each week. Study birds, make fish prints or go crab fishing. Registration not required but groups should call ahead. Also open select summer weekends, the lab is FREE due to grants from the Norris Foundation, Julius Sumner Miller Foundation, Kinder Morgan Foundation and Friends of CMA members.

HOURS: 3PM to 5PM Wed
PARKING: $7 at Cabrillo Beach
THOMAS GUIDE: 854 C2
KID-FRIENDLY * **WHEELCHAIR/STROLLER ACCESSIBLE**

Downey Museum of Art

10419 S Rives Ave, Downey 90241
562-861-0419
www.downeyca.org/visitor_museumart.php

The only art museum between Downtown LA and Long Beach specializes in the art of Southern California. The hundreds of items in the permanent collection and its rotating exhibits of local and national artists focus on modern and contemporary art. Located in Furman Park, the museum attracts school groups who go on "I Spy" missions to find certain elements in the displayed artwork. Providing a showcase of art to the area for 40 years, the museum is in the process of building a new facility.

HOURS: 1PM to 5PM Thu - Fri, call for seasonal hours
PARKING: FREE in lot/street * **THOMAS GUIDE:** 706 A3
KID-FRIENDLY * WHEELCHAIR/STROLLER ACCESSIBLE

Frederick R. Weisman Museum of Art

PEPPERDINE UNIVERSITY
24255 Pacific Coast Highway, Malibu 90263
310-506-7257
www.pepperdine.edu/cfa/weismanmuseum.htm

On the way to the beach, stop by this intimate art space on the rolling hills of the Pepperdine University campus. Part of the bustling Center for the Arts, the museum's 3,000 square feet of exhibit space annually hosts 8 to 10 temporary exhibitions of historic and contemporary art as well as student works.

HOURS: 11AM to 5PM Tue - Sun. and one hour before Center of the Arts performances.
PARKING: Obtain FREE pass at campus information booth
THOMAS GUIDE: 628 H7
WHEELCHAIR ACCESS

Frederick's of Hollywood Lingerie Museum

6608 Hollywood Blvd, Hollywood 90028
323-957-5953
www.fredericks.com

Glamorize yourself and visit an icon of Hollywood—
Frederick's—where starlets bought their underwear before
Victoria's Secret was chic. Frederick's has been the word
for sexy lingerie since Hollywood's golden days when glam-
our girls from Greta Garbo to Marilyn Monroe bought their
finest there. Established by Frederick Millenger, an East
Coast entrepreneur, the museum is located in his original
art deco store on Hollywood Blvd. Browse the sale items
then step in the back and up the stairs to the first Bra
Museum and the Celebrity Lingerie Hall of Fame. On display are Tom Hanks boxers from *Forest Gump,* Madonna's
black and gold bustier from her *Who's That Girl* tour and
the bra that Tony Curtis wore in *Some Like It Hot.*

HOURS: 10AM to 9PM Mon – Sat; 11AM to 6:30PM Sun
PARKING: Pay lots, metered street ★ **THOMAS GUIDE:** 593 E4

Griffith Observatory Satellite

4800 Western Heritage Way, LA 90027
323-664-1181
www.griffithobs.org

Zoom to the stars while waiting for the star atop Griffith
Park to come to life again. The park's long time landmark,
the 1935-built Griffith Observatory, is closed for renovation
until late 2005, but meanwhile the stars are shining at its
satellite location south of the LA Zoo in the park's northeast corner. In a temporary building, the satellite offers a
taste of what the "new" observatory will have. Astronomy
exhibits include a collection of meteorites, visuals of Mars

including an authentic Mars rock and a six-foot 3-D moon globe. You can still take in a planetarium show in the satellite's 21-foot planetarium theater. An astronomer points the way to Orion and other constellations using a projector and innovative night sky software. Get an outdoor close-up of the moon and distant planets using the telescope set up for public viewing with an astronomer providing guidance. Available each clear night from dark until 10PM.

HOURS: 1PM to 10PM Tue – Fri, 10AM to 10PM Sat & Sun, closed Mon
Planetarium Shows: 7PM to 9PM Fri, 1PM to 9PM Sat, 1PM to 5PM, Sun
PARKING: FREE Use south end of zoo lot and cross
Western Heritage Way to the satellite
THOMAS GUIDE: 564 B5
KID-FRIENDLY * **WHEELCHAIR/STROLLER ACCESS**

Hollywood Bowl Museum

2301 Highland Ave, Hollywood 90028
323-850-2058
www.hollywoodbowl.org

Learn about the rich history of LA's oldest and most famous musical landmark. Located steps from the Bowl, the museum exhibits a series of changing photographs, slide shows, memorabilia, and audio and video clips that span the Bowl's history from construction in 1921 until present day. Three terminals provide access to the Bowl's Intranet site, the Museum Resource Center, containing photos, audio and video samples, and past museum displays. Kids enjoy the "Come Make Noise" exhibit, where they can play and see demonstrations with stringed, percussive and keyboard instruments.

HOURS: 10AM to 8:30PM Tue – Sat and two hours before prior to concerts Sun eves, late June to late Sept. 10AM to 4:30PM Tue – Sat, late Sept to late June.
PARKING: FREE lot until 4:30PM * **THOMAS GUIDE:** 593 E4
KID-FRIENDLY * **HISTORIC**

Kenneth G. Fiske Museum of the Claremont Colleges

450 N College Way, Claremont 91711
909-621-8307
www.cuc.claremont.edu/fiske/

See the world's longest trumpet—seven feet—at one of the nation's most diverse collections of musical instruments. The museum holds more than 1,400 American, European and ethnic instruments from the 17th to the 20th centuries. View the earliest piano to come to California—made in Leipzig and shipped to Monterey about 1840. See Tibetan temple trumpets and a one-note flute made for Frederick the Great of Prussia. Located in the basement of Bridges Auditorium on the Pomona College campus, the museum also has one of the country's best brass collections.

HOURS: By appointment
PARKING: FREE * **THOMAS GUIDE:** 601 D3
KID-FRIENDLY (ages 6+) * **WHEELCHAIR/STROLLER ACCESSIBLE**

Korean Cultural Center

5505 Wilshire Blvd, LA 90036
323-936-7141
www.kccla.org

Explore 5,000 years of Korean history in this heritage center operated by the Korean government's Ministry of Culture and Tourism. Of note is a display of full-scale replicas of wall friezes found in the Seokguram Grotto Temple, an exhibit of a *sarangbang* or Korean scholar's study used by aristocrats 200 years ago and dramatic masks used in Korean theatrical storytelling.

HOURS: 9AM to 5PM Mon - Fri, 10AM to 1PM Sat
PARKING: FREE at back of building * **THOMAS GUIDE:** 633 D2
KID-FRIENDLY * **HISTORIC**

Los Angeles Fire Department Museum

1355 N Cahuenga Blvd, Hollywood 90028
323-464-2727
www.lafd.org/museum.htm

Visit old fire station number 27 and you may recognize it from a movie or two. Used as a backdrop in dozens of Hollywood films and television shows, the fully restored historic landmark is a tribute to the early years of LA's fire department. The museum features fire-fighting apparatus, equipment and memorabilia dating back to the 1800s. Staffed and curated by the LA Fire Department Historical Society (www.lafd.org/lafdhs.htm), the facility is one of three fire service museums in LA (all listed in this chapter). The society is also working on a memorial to fallen fire-fighters. Still in the construction stage, the memorial includes bronze statues of firefighters in action.

HOURS: 10AM to 4PM Sat
PARKING: Street * **THOMAS GUIDE:** 593 F5
KID-FRIENDLY * **HISTORIC** * **WHEELCHAIR/STROLLER ACCESS**

Manhattan Beach Historical Society Museum

1601 Manhattan Beach Blvd, Manhattan Beach 90266
310-374-7575
www.geocities.com/history90266/

Live life on the beach as it was at the turn of the 20th century when you visit this historic 1905 beach cottage in Polliwog Park. Staffed by volunteers of the Manhattan Beach Historical Society, the museum portion of the cottage is only open for a few weekend hours. View artifacts, photo displays, and old newspaper articles.

Headquartered here, the society holds monthly meetings that are FREE and open to the public.

HOURS: Noon to 3PM Sat - Sun
PARKING: Street * **THOMAS GUIDE:** 732 H6

Marine Mammal Care Center at Fort MacArthur

3601 S Gaffey St (at Leavenworth Dr), San Pedro 90731
310-548-5677
www.mar3ine.org

A sick or injured seal or seal lion stranded on LA's coast would perish without the efforts of this marine mammal "hospital." With a limited staff and dozens of volunteers, the care center tends to 40-50 patients. Often the hurt animals must be tube fed; rehabilitation can take up to three months or more. Once healthy, they are returned to the wild. Their care is made possible by the funding and dedication of MAR3INE (Marine Animal Rescue, Rehabilitation, and Release Into the Natural Environment). Visits to the rescue facility are on an informal basis. Getting to there is a bit tricky—turn right through Fort MacArthur's entrance at Angel's Gate Park. The center holds an annual Open House celebrating International Day of the Seal in March (see separate listing in March events chapter).

HOURS: 8AM to 4PM, daily
PARKING: FREE in lot * **THOMAS GUIDE:** 854 B2
KID-FRIENDLY * **WHEELCHAIR/STROLLER ACCESSIBLE**

Museum of Contemporary Art (MOCA) at the Pacific Design Center

8687 Melrose Ave, West Hollywood 90069
213-626-6222
www.moca.org

Located on the outdoor plaza of the Pacific Design Center, this branch of MOCA features contemporary architectural and design art from around the world. Recent exhibits have displayed Japanese graphic designers, Brazilian art, and photographs featuring interpretations of the home environment. The space also contains rotating exhibits from the permanent collection at the California Plaza location. FREE admission all days.

HOURS: 11AM to 5PM Tue & Wed, 11AM to 8PM Thu, 11AM to 5PM Fri, 11AM to 6PM Sat & Sun. Closed Mon, New Year's Day, Independence Day, Thanksgiving, and Christmas.
PARKING: Metered street parking
THOMAS GUIDE: 592 J7

Old Plaza Firehouse Museum

EL PUEBLO DE LOS ANGELES HISTORIC MONUMENT

125 Paseo de la Plaza (Olvera Street), LA 90012
213-628-3562
www.lacity.org/ELP/

Enter the oldest part of LA and visit one of the city's earliest fire stations. Built in 1884, the firehouse is one of the monument's 27 historic buildings and one of four that has been restored and turned into a museum. Housing firefighting equipment from the late 19th century, the small museum features a horse-drawn fire engine and a wall of firefighting hats. The historic building is one of three LA museums devoted to firefighting (all listed in this chapter) and one of 300 in the US.

HOURS: 10AM to 3PM, Tue - Sun
PARKING: Pay lot, metered street * **THOMAS GUIDE:** 634 G3
KID-FRIENDLY * HISTORIC * WHEELCHAIR/STROLLER ACCESS

The Bunny Museum

1933 Jefferson Dr, Pasadena 91104
626-798-8848
www.thebunnymuseum.com

Put on your bunny slippers and hop over to Steve Lubanski and Candace Frazee's house, which holds the Guinness Book of World Records for the largest collection of bunny stuff. The husband and wife bunny collectors live with all 17,000 bunny items – stuffed bunnies, ceramic bunnies, singing bunnies. And don't forget Bugs Bunny. Everything in their home is bunny-shaped—dishes, furniture, phones—even the toilet seat! Each item was a gift from one to the other. Oh, yes, there are six live bunnies that call this home, too. Stop by on major holidays—especially Easter, Halloween and Christmas—for extra kid-friendly bunny fun. Call for times. In October attend the FREE-admission Angel Festival founded by Candace where the museum sells angel bunnies (see March Events chapter).

HOURS: Year-round by appointment; Open House on major holidays
PARKING: Street * **THOMAS GUIDE:** 566 D1
KID-FRIENDLY * WHEELCHAIR/STROLLER ACCESSIBLE

The Getty Center

1200 Getty Center Dr, Los Angeles 90049
310-440-7300
www.getty.edu

The Getty is a 110-acre complex dedicated to the display, research, and conservation of the world's greatest art. The six travertine, glass, and metal buildings house a museum, research institute, library, and auditorium that gleam from their hilltop location in the Santa Monica Mountains. The museum, consisting of five interconnected pavilions, hosts one of the most prestigious art collections in the world, featuring pre-20th century European paintings, decorative arts, old master drawings, Medieval and Renaissance manuscripts, and 20th century photographs. Famed paintings by Monet, Rembrandt, Van Gogh and Renoir are displayed. The grounds are highlighted by spectacular gardens and magnificent city views. FREE concerts, films, seminars and lectures are held in the 450-seat Williams Auditorium (see Web site for schedule). An 800,000-volume research library is available to scholars and the public. Kids enjoy the Family Room (hands-on activities), Art Adventures for Families (gallery games) and Art Kits.

PARKING: $5 structure. MTA bus line 71 serves the Getty.
THOMAS GUIDE: 631 G1
KID-FRIENDLY * WHEELCHAIR/STROLLER ACCESS

UCLA Fowler Museum of Cultural History

UCLA CAMPUS
405 Hilgard Ave, LA 90095
310-825-4361
www.fowler.ucla.edu

Although it holds over 150,000 pieces of artwork, the Fowler defines itself as a museum of culture, not just art. While it displays ancient and modern art from Africa, Asia, Oceania and the Americas, this museum's origins and distinctiveness come from its over 600,000 archeological objects taken from digs throughout the 20th century. The museum's first and largest gift was the Sir Henry Wellcome Collection of 30,000 African and Oceanic pieces assembled in the early 20th century and donated in 1965. Since then, the Fowler has assembled impressive collections of African textiles, Mexican and other Latin American folk art, pre-Columbian ceramics, Eskimo art, and European silver from the workshops of such noted craftsmen as Paul Revere and Karl Fabergé. The museum enhances its art and artifacts with lectures and symposiums on its current exhibits as well as plays, live music and dance that celebrate the cultures featured here. School and group tours are FREE.

HOURS: Noon to 5PM Wed – Sun, Noon to 8PM Thu. Closed Mon & Tue
Campus parking $7, use lot #4 off Sunset Blvd. at Westwood Plaza
THOMAS GUIDE: 632 B2

Wells Fargo History Museum

333 S Grand Ave, LA 90071
213-253-7166
www.wellsfargohistory.com

More than 150 years ago Henry Wells and William G. Fargo founded an American legend that included a bank, express delivery of real gold and a stagecoach company. The red 2,500-lb horse-drawn coaches crafted in Concord, NH continue to be the finance company's symbol. Made by Abbott-Downing, each coach was individually numbered. See number 599 that rolled through southern Kentucky from 1897 to 1915 at this downtown Wells Fargo museum, one of several in the West. Gaze at the 100-ounce gold Challenge Nugget, walk inside a historically re-created agent's office and view a panoramic painting of LA as it looked in 1852.

HOURS: 9AM to 5PM Mon - Fri
PARKING: Metered street, pay lots * **THOMAS GUIDE:** 634 F4
KID-FRIENDLY * **HISTORIC**

William S. Hart Park Ranch & Museum

24151 San Fernando Rd, Newhall 91321
661-259-0855 (Park)
661-254-4584 (Museum)
www.hartmuseum.org

Cowboy fans, take Hart. The Spanish Colonial-style mansion at this Newhall attraction served as home to silent film star and director William S. Hart, known as "Two Gun Bill." Visitors can let their imagination wander as they inspect the home's original furnishings including western art, Native American artifacts and memorabilia from Hollywood's early days. Known as "The Horseshoe Ranch," the 260-acre site includes a furnished ranch house open for self-guided tours, a dog cemetery, a gift shop and picnic facilities. Children delight in the ranch's live farm animals exhibit and for 25 cents they can purchase food pellets to feed goats and other barnyard inhabitants. A herd of bison, descended from a handful donated by Walt Disney Studios in 1962, also roams here. FREE guided tours.

HOURS: Tours 11AM to 3:30PM Wed – Sun, mid-June to Labor Day; 10AM to 12:30PM Wed – Fri and 11AM to 3:30PM Sat & Sun, mid-Sept to mid-June.
PARKING: FREE * **THOMAS GUIDE:** 4641 A2
KID-FRIENDLY * **HISTORIC**

MUSEUMS WITH FREE DAYS

Craft and Folk Art Museum

5814 Wilshire Blvd, LA 90036
323-937-4230
www.cafam.org

Eye-popping colors from Japanese puppets to Mexican silverwork to African masks greet visitors at this collection of traditional and modern arts & crafts and folk art. Started in 1965 as The Egg and the Eye by collectors Edith and Frank Wyle, the museum also stages the popular International Festival of Masks held across the street in Hancock Park (see October Events chapter). Now in a partnership with the City of LA Cultural Affairs Department, the museum offers FREE family art workshops and hosts open houses for new exhibitions throughout the year.

FREE: 1st Wed every month
REGULAR ADMISSION: $3.50 adults, $2.50 students/seniors, FREE ages 12 and under
HOURS: 11AM to 5PM Wed - Sun
PARKING: Metered street, pay lots ✳ **THOMAS GUIDE:** 633 C2
KID-FRIENDLY ✳ **WHEELCHAIR/STROLLER ACCESS**

Huntington Library, Art Collections, and Botanical Gardens

1151 Oxford Road, San Marino 91108
626- 405-2100
www.huntington.org

Aspire to the elegant life and respire to the elevated air of this estate turned museum. Promenade through the lawns and gardens that railroad magnate Henry Huntington began cultivating over 100 years ago. Explore the desert, rose, camellia, jungle or Shakespeare gardens. In between the statuary admire rare and endangered botanical species or meditate in the Zen and bonsai courts. Explore the Library Exhibition Halls, with its display of rare books. Huntington, father of LA's Pacific Electric Railway known as the "Red Cars," was a big book collector. View early editions of Shakespeare's masterpieces, a Gutenberg Bible and a stunning edition of Audubon's *Bird's of America.* British and Continental art offers a slice of the life between the American and French revolutions. The collection, including Gainsborough's *Blue Boy* and Lawrence's *Pinkie,* is housed within the Huntington Gallery, originally the Huntington home. Before discovering further cultural treasures, catch your breath at the Rose Garden Tea Room (reservations required!) or the more casual Café.

FREE: 1st Thu every month
REGULAR ADMISSION: $12.50 adults, $10 ages 65+,
$8.50 students ages 12 - 18 or with full-time student ID,
$5 ages 5 – 11, FREE ages under 5
HOURS: (Sept 1 to May 31) Noon to 4:30PM Tue – Fri,
10:30AM to 4:30PM Sat – Sun;
(June 1 to Aug 31) 10:30PM to 4:30PM Tue – Sun
PARKING: FREE * **THOMAS GUIDE:** 566 D7
KID-FRIENDLY
WHEELCHAIR/STROLLER ACCESS (pick up the FREE color-coded map
for best access)

The Japanese American National Museum

369 E First St, LA 90012

213-625-0414

www.janm.org

Discover the history of the Nisei, first generation Japanese Americans, at the only museum in the US dedicated to preserving and sharing the experience of being an American with Japanese ancestry. Learn about the pioneering *Issei*, Japanese immigrants, who built the original building the museum utilizes—the Nishi *Hongwanji* Buddhist Temple. Once a hub of religious and social activity in Little Tokyo, the temple was used to store belongings of Japanese sent to internment camps during World War II. Abandoned, the ornate 1925 temple later became the keystone of the museum after a massive renovation and restoration. Much of Japanese American history was lost during the War due to the internment. The museum works to recover that history and promote a community interest in Japanese heritage. Check the museum calendar for special events and classes (some FREE some with a fee) such as *taiko* drum sessions, crafting *sakura* (pop-up) cards and making *origami* (paper folding).

FREE: 3rd Thu every month
REGULAR ADMISSION: $6 adults, $5 seniors & students with ID,
$3 ages 6-17, FREE ages 5 and under
HOURS: 10AM to 8PM, last admission at 7:30PM
PARKING: Pay lots, usually less than $5 in adjacent areas
THOMAS GUIDE: 634 G4
KID-FRIENDLY * **WHEELCHAIR ACCESS/STROLLERS ACCESS** if not crowded

Long Beach Museum of Art

2300 E Ocean Blvd, Long Beach 90803

562-439-2119

www.lbma.org

No other LA-area museum has the breathtaking outdoor views this one does—on a bluff overlooking the Pacific Ocean and the Long Beach Harbor. One of the museum's main collections is centered on 300 years of American decorative art objects, including furnishings and accessories. An apt choice for a museum that uses a renovated 1912 Craftsman home—the historic Elizabeth Milbank Anderson house—and a carriage house—as part of its facilities. The museum also exhibits early 20th century European art, California modernism and contemporary California art. In addition to 5,000 paintings, sculptures, drawings, works on paper and decorative art objects, the museum has archived 3,000 artists' videos. A welcoming institution, it hosts several on-going events for visitors including Twilight Thursdays with workshops and music in the galleries and FREE appetizers and drink specials in the café. The museum offers FREE family art-making workshops the second Sunday of every month and a FREE Children's Cultural Festival in September or October (see October Events chapter).

FREE: 1st Fri every month
REGULAR ADMISSION: $5 adults, $4 seniors 62+ & students, FREE for ages 12 and under
HOURS: 11AM to 5PM Tue - Sun, closed Mon
PARKING: FREE in museum lot on Ocean Blvd, one block west of the museum
THOMAS GUIDE: 825 G1
KID-FRIENDLY * HISTORIC * WHEELCHAIR/STROLLER ACCESS

LA County Museum of Art (LACMA)

5905 Wilshire Blvd, LA 90036
323-857-6000
www.lacma.org

Boasting over 100,000 works of art in five buildings, LACMA is the largest visual arts museum in the Western

US. Its collections span time from ancient to modern yet reflect the multi-cultural aspects of today's Southern California. The permanent collections include American, Asian, Islamic, and Latin American paintings and sculptures, as well as decorative arts, costumes, textiles, photography and drawings. Innovative traveling exhibitions, music programs, film events and art education programs for adults and children supplement the permanent collections. Founded in 1910 as part of Exposition Park's Museum of Science, History and Art, LACMA collected much of its best-known art—Ancient Egyptian, Medieval, Renaissance, and Baroque—in the mid-1940s. It moved to its current Miracle Mile home in 1965.

FREE: 2nd Tue each month and after 5PM daily
REGULAR ADMISSION: $9 adults, $5 ages 62+ and students 18+ with ID, FREE for ages 17 and under.
HOURS: Noon to 8PM Mon, Tue, Thu; Noon to 9PM Fri;
11AM to 8PM Sat – Sun. Closed Wed, Thanksgiving, Christmas Day
PARKING: Pay lots at Wilshire Blvd & Spaulding Ave and at Wilshire and Ogden Dr; fees vary; parking is FREE after 7PM.
Very limited metered street parking
THOMAS GUIDE: 633 B2
KID-FRIENDLY * WHEELCHAIR/STROLLER ACCESS

MAK Center for Art and Architecture

835 N Kings Rd, West Hollywood 90069
323-651-1510
www.makcenter.org

"The sense for the perception of architecture is not the eyes —but living." Thus said famed architect Rudolf Schindler whose landmark Schindler House serves as the home for the MAK Center, a sanctuary for boundary-challenging architects and artists. The house is an example of "space architecture" and its flat roof and open design are hallmarks of the California Style of Design. The house and other nearby buildings designed by Schindler serve as inspiration for risk-taking artists and architects whose drawings, texts, photography, sculpture, installations and film are displayed at the MAK Center. Supported by the Republic of Austria and Friends of the Schindler House, the MAK also holds frequent symposiums, lectures, performances, and workshops at the house and at other sites. MAK also features live modern and experimental music.

FREE: Fridays 4PM to 6PM and all day Sept 10 and Dec 1
REGULAR ADMISSION: $5 per person, FREE for ages 12 and under
HOURS: 11AM to 6PM Wed – Sun, closed Mon – Tue
TOURS: On the half-hour, 11:30PM to 2:30PM Sat - Sun
PARKING: Limited metered and FREE street,
pay parking at city garage at Santa Monica Blvd and Kings Rd
THOMAS GUIDE: 593 A6
KID-FRIENDLY

Museum of Contemporary Art (MOCA)

CALIFORNIA PLAZA
250 S Grand Ave, LA 90012
213-626-6222
www.moca.org

If you like your art noisy, electric, animated, controversial, and most of all, challenging, MOCA is for you. Displaying contemporary art from 1940-present, this museum contains over 5,000 works including abstract expressionism, pop art, minimalist, and post-minimalist art. You'll find paintings, sculpture, photography, drawings, and mixed media including pieces by famed artists like Pollock, Hockney, Ruscha, DeKooning and Arbus. The Indian red sandstone building, designed by Arata Isozaki, uses pyramid skylights, glass cubes, and cylinders to create an environment with the right light, color and space to house the quirky art. Lectures provide background on current exhibits and family workshops give kids insight into non-traditional art. The museum is FREE all day Thursday through the generosity of Wells Fargo.

FREE: 11AM to 8PM Thu
REGULAR ADMISSION: $8 adults, $5 ages 65+ & students with ID,
FREE ages 12 and under
HOURS: 11AM to 5PM Mon & Fri, 11AM – 8PM Thu,
11AM to 6PM Sat & Sun. Closed Tue, Wed, New Year's Day,
Independence Day, Thanksgiving, and Christmas.
PARKING: Metered street, $10 maximum at Hope St and Kosciuszko Way
THOMAS GUIDE: 634 F3
WHEELCHAIR ACCESS

MOCA at the Geffen Contemporary

152 N Central Ave, LA 90012
213-626-6222
www.moca.org

Looking for nostalgic farmscapes or luminous still lifes? Keep looking. This space, formerly known as the Temporary Contemporary, is home to massive, industrial-strength, powerful installation art, constructions, and sculptures. The museum is in a former warehouse and police car service garage converted by Frank Gehry into a space that holds artwork too big for MOCA's California Plaza facility. The art is thought provoking, controversial, and emotional. And not a Thomas Kinkade in sight. The museum is FREE all day Thursday through the generosity of Wells Fargo.

FREE: 11AM to 8PM Thu
REGULAR ADMISSION: $8 adults, $5 ages 65+ & students with ID, FREE
ages 12 and under
HOURS: 11AM to 5PM Mon & Fri, 11AM – 8PM Thu,
11AM to 6PM Sat & Sun. Closed Tue, Wed, New Year's Day,
Independence Day, Thanksgiving, and Christmas.
PARKING: $3 at lot on First St & Central Ave * **THOMAS GUIDE:** 634 G4
WHEELCHAIR ACCESS

Museum of Neon Art

501 W Olympic Blvd, LA 90015
213-489-9918
www.neonmona.org

Have a de-light-ful time perusing this funky collection of colorful art made from gas-filled glass tubing. The only permanent neon museum in the world, this collection spotlights both the practical and the whimsical with streetlights and advertising signs sharing space with sculptures of light in the form of people, animals and abstract shapes. Sculptures range from a depiction of the Mona Lisa—the MONA museum's namesake—to animated signs that once graced now-defunct hotels. Exhibits also trace the history and explain the technology of this unique art form. The museum offers three-hour nighttime double-decker bus tours of neon signs of LA. ($45) and eight-week neon sign making classes ($450).

FREE: 5PM to 8PM 2nd Thu every month
REGULAR ADMISSION: $5 adults, $3.50 students ages 13 to 22 with ID and seniors ages 65+: FREE for ages under 12.
HOURS: 11AM to 5PM Wed – Sat; Noon to 5PM, Sun; 11AM to 8PM, 2nd Thu every month. Closed Mon, Tue and major holidays
PARKING: FREE in Renaissance Tower garage on Grand Ave, south of 9th St; metered parking on Olympic Blvd, FREE on Sun
THOMAS GUIDE: 634 E5
KID-FRIENDLY

Museum of Jurassic Technology

9341 Venice Blvd, Culver City 90232
310-836-6131
www.mjt.org

After sipping an early evening latte in Culver City on Thursday night, sprint over to this museum and take advantage of the 15 minutes of FREE admission. That's right—a quarter of an hour. Get there early enough so you're at the door at the stroke of 7:45PM. And unlike most museums, you have to ring a doorbell to gain entry. Prepare to be baffled, for few can explain what the museum is really about. Its exhibits contain an unusual assortment of curiosities, seemingly related to science, several related to botanical science. Your mind will wonder as to whether the exhibits are science, art, or what?

FREE: 7:45PM to 8PM Thu, 5:45PM to 6PM Fri - Sun
REGULAR ADMISSION: (suggested) $5 adults, $3 ages 12 to 21, students with ID, seniors age 60+ and those unemployed, $2 disabled and military personnel in uniform, FREE for ages 12 and under.
HOURS: 2PM to 8PM Thu, Noon to 6PM Fri — Sun. Closed Mon — Wed and major holidays.
PARKING: Metered street * **THOMAS GUIDE:** 672 G1
WHEELCHAIR/STROLLER ACCESS

Museum of Latin American Art

628 Alamitos Ave, Long Beach 90802
562-437-1689
www.molaa.org

MoLAA is the only museum in the US to exclusively exhibit contemporary Latin American art. Located in the East Village Arts District of Long Beach, the museum galleries are housed in what once was a popular roller skating rink, The Hippodrome. Built in the roaring '20s, The Hippodrome was a skaters sanctuary for 40 years and its vaulted ceilings and wooden floors make it a perfect match for displaying art. MoLAA is "more than just a museum." It promotes itself as a cultural center offering live entertainment, inspiring programs and a hip restaurant, Viva, that features authentic Latin American cuisine.

FREE: 11:30AM to 7PM Fri
REGULAR ADMISSION: $5 adults, $3 seniors & students with ID, FREE for ages 12 and under
HOURS: 11:30AM to 7PM Tue – Fri, 11AM to 7PM Sat, 11AM to 6PM Sun. Closed Mon, Thanksgiving, Christmas, New Year's Day

PARKING: FREE * **THOMAS GUIDE:** 795 F7
KID-FRIENDLY * **WHEELCHAIR/STROLLER ACCESS**

Museum of the American West

4700 Western Heritage Way, LA 90027
323-667-2000
www.museumoftheamericanwest.org

Hitch up the wagon, pardner, and make tracks for the junction of the Golden State and Ventura Freeways where you'll find one of the nation's largest museums of its kind. Formerly the Autry Museum of Western Heritage, this museum is dedicated to legendary radio and television star Gene Autry's dream of preserving and displaying Western history and art, as well as recounting the stories of settlers and their descendents who changed and were changed by the American West. Nine galleries display over 78,000 objects including paintings, pottery, photographs, quilts, clothing, and other artwork and artifacts. Recent special exhibitions have illustrated the less-known contributions of women, Native Americans, Chinese and Jews to the saga of the Old West. If you're bringing the young'uns, mosey on over to the McCormick Tribune Foundation Gallery for pioneer-related games and workshops.

FREE: 4PM to 8PM every Thu
REGULAR ADMISSION: $7.50 adults, $5 ages 60+ & students, $3 ages 2-12
HOURS: 10AM to 5PM Tue – Sun. Closed most Mon but open Martin Luther King Day, President's Day, Memorial Day, Labor Day, and New Year's Day. Closed Thanksgiving and Christmas Day.
PARKING: FREE lot * **THOMAS GUIDE:** 564 B4
KID-FRIENDLY * **WHEELCHAIR/STROLLER ACCESS**

Natural History Museum of Los Angeles County

900 Exposition Blvd, LA 90007
213-763-DINO
www.nhm.org

Enter into one of *FREE L.A.'s* favorite places to hang out—
LA's second oldest cultural institution and the largest natural and historical museum in the West. The venerable old
building built in 1913 with its wide sweeping marble stair-
cases holds 33 million artifacts. The three floors of permanent exhibits include rare dinosaurs and fossils, giant dio-
ramas of preserved African and American mammals, an
interactive bird hall and marine animals. The Ralph M.
Parsons Discovery Center features live snakes, fish and
lizards and the largest live Insect Zoo in the West. Kids can
spend hours making fossil rubbings, touching animal pelts
and handling nature specimens here. The Gem & Mineral
Hall literally glitters with gems and the largest collection of
gold in the US. Take a step back in time and view artifacts
from Native American and Pre-Columbian cultures, and
California and Southwest history plus early Hollywood
memorabilia. The museum hosts several new exhibits and
events each year.

FREE: 1st Tue every month
REGULAR ADMISSION: $9 adults, $6.50 students 18+ with ID/seniors
62+ and ages 13 – 17, $2 ages 5 – 12, FREE for ages 5 and under.
HOURS: 9:30AM to 5PM Mon – Fri, 10AM to 5PM Sat & Sun,
closed Independence Day, Thanksgiving Day, Christmas Day,
and New Year's Day
PARKING: Pay lot on Menlo Ave, just south of Exposition Blvd and east
of Vermont Ave. Fee is usually $5 unless other events are happening
in the Exposition Park area. Handicap parking spaces in both
museum parking lots are FREE.
THOMAS GUIDE: 674 B1
KID-FRIENDLY * **HISTORIC** * **WHEELCHAIR/STROLLER ACCESS**

Norton Simon Museum

411 W Colorado Blvd, Pasadena 91105
626-449-6840
www.nortonsimon.org

Visit distant lands on the same corner where Tournament of Roses Queens blow their opening kisses on New Years Day. Architect Frank Gehry redesigned the modern two-story building in 1999 while landscape designer Nancy Goslee Power revamped the museum gardens. The pond full of water lilies is suggestive of Claude Monet's garden in Giverny, France. Monet's influence is inside as well as out, with his paintings sharing space with Van Goghs, Rembrandts and Picassos. The downstairs gallery is filled with ancient ivory, bronze and stone sculptures from India and Southeast Asia. A family audio tour, recommended for ages 7+ is available for $3.

FREE: 6PM to 9PM 1st Fri every month
REGULAR ADMISSION: $6 adults, $3 ages 62+,
FREE for ages 18 and under & students with ID.
HOURS: Noon to 6PM Mon, Wed, Thu, Sat, Sun; Noon to 9PM Fri.
Closed Tue, New Year's Day, Thanksgiving, Christmas Day.
PARKING: FREE * **THOMAS GUIDE:** 565 G5
KID-FRIENDLY (ages 6+) * **WHEELCHAIR ACCESS**

Pacific Asia Museum

46 N Los Robles, Pasadena 91101
626-669-2742
www.pacificasiamuseum.org

Past the bronze dragons, enter the Imperial Chinese palace-styled courtyard and discover a more detailed version of the Pacific Rim. The courtyard features Oriental figures, landscaping and a koi pond, while within the museum the permanent collection spans 5,000 years of Asian and Pacific Island art and artifacts, including breathtakingly delicate Chinese ceramics. During the year FREE

Family Festival Days celebrate traditional holidays from a variety of cultures: Korean, Philippine, Japanese. These special days often offer workshops, entertainment, even snacks of the celebrated culture.

FREE: Family Festival Days, dates vary
REGULAR ADMISSION: $7 adults, $5 students & seniors
HOURS: 10AM to 5PM Mon, Thu, Sat, Sun; 10AM to 8PM Fri
PARKING: FREE in museum lot * **THOMAS GUIDE:** 565 J4
KID-FRIENDLY * WHEELCHAIR/STROLLER ACCESS

Page Museum at the La Brea Tar Pits

5801 Wilshire Blvd, LA 90036
323-934-PAGE
www.tarpits.org

Visit the museum home of the Rancho La Brea Tar Pits and discover what exactly that black bubbling ooze is all about. Learn what LA was really like between 10,000 and 40,000 years ago, during the region's last Ice Age. The Tar Pits are considered to have the largest and most diverse fossilized parts of Ice Age plants and animals including mammoths, saber-toothed cats, giant sloths and and dire wolves. Since 1906, more than one million bones have been recovered with the Page Museum having about three million of them. During the summer you can watch paleontologists pry remains from the sticky asphalt in Excavation Pit 91 for FREE. Inside the museum you can watch scientists and volunteers carefully brush, wipe and scrape the gunk off fossils in a glass-enclosed research lab that lets visitors peer inside.

FREE: 1st Tue every month
REGULAR ADMISSION: $7 adults, $4.50 ages 62+ & students with ID, $2 ages 5-12 years, FREE for ages 5 and under.
Hours: 9:30AM to 5PM Mon – Fri, 10AM to 5PM Sat - Sun & holidays, closed Independence Day, Thanksgiving Day, Christmas Day, and New Year's Day.

PARKING: $6 with Page Museum validation
(Page Museum parking lot only), $8 otherwise
THOMAS GUIDE: 633 C2
KID-FRIENDLY * **WHEELCHAIR/STROLLER ACCESS**

Pasadena Museum of California Art

490 E Union St, Pasadena 91101
626-568-3665
www.pmcaonline.org

Explore 8,000 square feet dedicated to the dynamic elements of Californian art, architecture and design, dating from the mid 19th century to the present. Relatively new, the museum's own architecture is an aesthetic pleasure, from the natural light which enhances the open staircase to the rooftop terrace which takes advantage of Pasadena's beautiful vistas. Exhibits strive to place creative Californians in an international and national context, while highlighting their experimentation, innovation and creativity.

FREE: 5PM to 8PM, 1st Fri of every month
REGULAR ADMISSION: $6 adults, $4 ages 65+ and students with ID.
FREE for ages 12 and under
HOURS: 10AM to 5PM, Wed – Sun; 10AM to 8PM Fri
PARKING: Fee in public structure or lot * **THOMAS GUIDE:** 565 J4
WHEELCHAIR ACCESS

Skirball Cultural Center

2701 N Sepulveda Blvd, LA 90049
310-440-4500
www.skirball.org

More than a museum, the Skirball Cultural Center is a tribute to nearly every facet of Jewish religion and culture. The center presents Judaism in its relationships with the

American political, social, political, economic and religious environment. The core exhibit, entitled *Jewish Life from Antiquity to America,* displays artifacts, symbols, and models of the celebrations of holidays and life cycle events from Biblical times until present day. Docent-led tours last from 20 minutes to an hour and group tours are available on request in several languages. Lectures, film, theater, and music programs augment the exhibits, although many of these programs require a separate admission charge. FREE gallery kits for families with kids 3-8 contain museum-related games, puzzles and clues for the daily treasure hunt. The center has a restaurant and shop on site.

FREE: Dec 25 & 26
REGULAR ADMISSION: $8 adults, $6 seniors & students, FREE for ages 12 and under
HOURS: Noon to 5PM Tue – Sat, 11AM to 5PM Sun, closed Mon
PARKING: $5 lot * **THOMAS GUIDE:** 591 F1
WHEELCHAIR/STROLLER ACCESS

UCLA Hammer Museum

10899 Wilshire Blvd at Westwood Blvd, LA 90024
310-443-7000
www.hammer.ucla.edu

Located just off campus in Westwood Village, the museum's 14,000 square feet bridges classical art with contemporary works. Opened in 1990 as a showcase of former Occidental Petroleum Chairman Armand Hammer's personal collection of old master paintings and drawings, the museum's fate fell into limbo after he died 3 weeks later. Now managed by UCLA, the museum exhibits Hammer's permanent collection, primarily Impressionist and post-Impressionist paintings by artists such as Cassatt, Monet and Van Gogh. The museum also rotates displays from Hammer's collection of Honore Daumier and contemporaries. Woven in the mix are temporary exhibitions of under represented and contemporary artists from all fields of visual arts. Above the museum, in the same building, is the Grunwald Center for the Graphic Arts, housing 45,000 prints, photos, drawings and artists' books from the Renaissance to today. Serving as a cultural meeting place as well as a curated museum, UCLA Hammer offers lectures, workshops and readings (see Halloween Events chapter) and holds several performances in its open-air courtyard.

FREE: 11AM to 9PM Thu
REGULAR ADMISSION: $5 adults, $3 ages 65+, FREE UCLA students, faculty and staff
HOURS: 11AM to 7PM Tue, Wed, Fri, Sat; 11AM to 9PM Thu; 11AM to 5PM Sun; closed Mon
PARKING: Under the museum, $2.75 for first 3 hours with museum stamp; $1.50 for each additional 20 minutes; $3 flat rate after 6:30PM Thu. Parking for people with disabilities on levels P1 and P3.
THOMAS GUIDE: 632 B3
WHEELCHAIR ACCESS

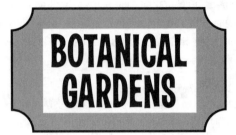

Brand Park Memory Garden

15174 San Fernando Mission Blvd, Mission Hills 91345
888-LA-PARKS or 213-473-7070
www.laparks.org

Memories of all 20 California missions are planted here—literally. The area now known as Brand Park once served as the gardens for the Mission San Fernando de Rey de España, simply called the San Fernando Mission. Part of the original mission land grant, the park's Memory Garden contains flowers and shrubs from the rest of the state's missions. A designated California Historic Landmark, the gardens offer a quiet repose from the park's bustling baseball diamond.

ADMISSION: FREE ★ **HOURS:** Sunrise to sunset
PARKING: FREE ★ **THOMAS GUIDE:** 501 H2
KID-FRIENDLY ★ **WHEELCHAIR/STROLLER ACCESS**

Castaic Lake Water Agency Conservatory Garden

27234 Bouquet Canyon Rd, Santa Clarita 91350
661-297-1600
www.clwa.org/Conservatory.htm

How does your garden grow? Experts at the Water Conservatory Garden and Learning Center put their green thumbs to work to produce a lavish display of plants. The 7-acre garden features 350+ varieties of plants, including lantana, sedum and verbena. Assorted grasses and 1,500 roses also enhance this landscaped Santa Clarita setting. Visitors learn about ways to conserve water by planting foliage suitable for the Southern California environment. Educational programs explain that although two-thirds of the Earth is covered by water only one-third of 1 percent can be used by consumers. Garden displays and hands-on demonstrations teach visitors about soil preparation, irrigation systems, mulches, plant zoning, microclimates and slope stabilization.

ADMISSION: FREE * **HOURS:** 9AM to 2PM Mon – Fri
PARKING: FREE, adjacent to the Rio Vista Water Treatment Plant. Turn in at the Central Park signal in Saugus, turn left and go to the top of the hill.
THOMAS GUIDE: 4461 A7
KID-FRIENDLY * WHEELCHAIR/STROLLER ACCESS

Chavez Ravine Arboretum

ELYSIAN PARK

1880 Academy Dr at Stadium Way, LA 90012
213-485-5054 (Arboretum Maintenance)
888-LA-PARKS or 213-473-7070
www.laparks.org

Founded 100+ years ago by the LA Horticultural Society, the arboretum is LA's first botanical garden and is nestled in the city's oldest public park. A global tribute to trees, many of them rare, most of the original trees planted from the 1890s to the 1920s are still standing. Declared an LA Historic Cultural Monument in 1967, Chavez Ravine contains more than 1,000 varieties of trees from around the world. Many of them are the oldest and largest of their kind in California and even the US. The trees are numbered based on their species and the park department's Web site has a downloadable guide that matches the number with their horticultural name. Located north of Dodger Stadium, you'll find it on the west side of Stadium Way. Spot the sign for the Grace E. Simons Lodge and turn in.

ADMISSION: FREE * **HOURS:** Sunrise to Sunset
PARKING: Metered street, limited FREE in lot * **THOMAS GUIDE:** 594 G6
KID-FRIENDLY

Earl Burns Miller Japanese Garden

CAL STATE UNIVERSITY LONG BEACH
1250 N Bellflower Blvd, Long Beach 90822
562-985-8885

Meditate in the small, but tranquil setting of this campus hideaway. Dedicated in 1981, the 1.5-acre garden was created in memory of Earl Burns Miller and funded by his wife, Mrs. Loraine Miller Collins. All of the garden elements, from the cedar wood gate to a small lake and tiny island, are modeled after gardens in Japan. Several stone ornaments, including a large Kasuga lantern, were imported from Japan. Enter the college oasis through a tiled roof gateway guarded by two traditional *Komo-Inu* or Lion Dogs that ward off evil spirits. A full color self-guided tour brochure costs $1 at the garden cart.

ADMISSION: FREE unless a special program is offered
HOURS: 8AM to 3:30PM Tue to Fri, Noon to 4PM Sun. Closed mid-Dec to Jan 31, the week before Easter, July 4th, Thanksgiving day through following Sun. Dates vary.

PARKING: Metered space or paid day pass;
students spaces FREE Noon to 4PM Sun
THOMAS GUIDE: 796 C6

Exposition Rose Garden

701 State Dr, LA 90037
213-748-4772
www.laparks.org

On the National Register of Historic Places, this 7.5-acre sunken bed of roses blooms March to November. A popular wedding locale (reservations and fee required), the garden features 9,000 rose bushes and 140+ varieties. A one-time horse track turned perennial garden, everything has been coming up roses at this urban oasis since 1927 when local nurseries donated the bushes. The originals are gone but there are varieties dating from the 1940s and 1950s, including a Queen Anne that is more than 50-years-old. Look for the Blooming of the Roses Festival in April (see April Events chapter).

ADMISSION: FREE
HOURS: 9AM to sunset, daily. Closed Jan 1 to Mar 15 for pruning and renovation.
PARKING: Pay lot, metered street * **THOMAS GUIDE:** 674 B2
KID-FRIENDLY * HISTORIC * WHEELCHAIR/STROLLER ACCESSIBLE

Fern Dell

GRIFFITH PARK
4730 Crystal Springs Dr, LA 90027
323-913-4688
www.laparks.org

Relax in one of the smallest natural gardens you'll find in the city. Tucked away in Griffith Park, the nation's largest municipal park is an area shaded by hundreds of leafy ferns—hence the name Fern Dell. Offering a wonderful respite from the summer heat, the cool haven has bubbling brooks, little waterfalls and flowers. A Gabrieleno Indian Site at Fern Dell is an official LA Historic Cultural Monument. Located west of Los Feliz Blvd & Riverside Dr, the entrance to the made-in-the-shade space is through Western Ave.

ADMISSION: FREE * **HOURS:** Sunrise to 6:30PM
PARKING: FREE * **THOMAS GUIDE:** 564 C7
KID-FRIENDLY * **HISTORIC**

James Irvine Garden

JAPANESE AMERICAN CULTURAL & COMMUNITY CENTER
244 S San Pedro St, LA 90012
213-628-2725
www.jaccc.org

Find sanctuary in this tiny oasis in the city. Only one-quarter of an acre, the Japanese-style garden is on a sub-level of the Japanese American Community & Cultural Center. You have to take an elevator to access it but when the doors open an enchanting place is revealed. Also called *Seiryu-en* or "Garden of The Clear Stream," a running 170-foot stream does wind through the lush sunken garden. Tall trees block out the city so you can hear the sounds of the waterway that's edged with boulders from Mt. Baldy. A waterfall cascades over one of those rocks and arched bridges provide pathways over the water. Hundreds of Japanese gardeners, landscape contractors, nurserymen and other volunteers created the garden in the 1970s and continue to maintain it. The American Association of Nurserymen gave it the National Landscape Award in 1981.

ADMISSION: FREE * **HOURS:** 9AM to 5PM daily, closed certain holidays
PARKING: Pay lots * **THOMAS GUIDE:** 634 G4
KID-FRIENDLY * **WHEELCHAIR ACCESS:** Limited

LA County Arboretum and Botanic Garden

301 N Baldwin Ave, Arcadia 91007
626-821-3222
www.arboretum.org

A movie location favorite, this 127-acre living museum features plants, flowers and trees from every continent except Antarctica. A hub for horticultural education, the arboretum has 20,000 permanent plantings, 5,000 species and varieties from 200+ countries, and has introduced 100+ plants to Southern California. Strutting peacocks wander around the garden's sections planted by region. The arboretum's jungle-like atmosphere has changed since it opened in 1948. Gone dry from drought and water conservation is Baldwin Lake where Johnny Weissmuller once swam across the water as Tarzan and Jungle Jim. Meanwhile, Meyberg Waterfall still flows, conserving and recycling 40,000 gallons of water every hour. Take a peek inside the historic Queen Anne Cottage, a Victorian house built circa 1885 by Lucky Baldwin. Also on site: the Hugo Reid Adobe circa 1835-1840 and the old Santa Anita Depot.

ADMISSION: FREE 3rd Tue every month
REGULAR ADMISSION: $6 adults, $4 ages 62+, $4 students with ID, $1.50 ages 5-12, FREE ages under 5
HOURS: 9AM to 5PM daily, closed Dec 25
PARKING: FREE * **THOMAS GUIDE:** 567 A1
KID-FRIENDLY * HISTORIC * WHEELCHAIR/STROLLER ACCESS

LA River Center & Gardens

CALIFORNIA BUILDING
570 W Ave 26 (at San Fernando Rd), LA 90065
323-221-9944
www.smmc.ca.gov

Renewal in action epitomizes this blossoming environmental showcase that encourages the community to go beyond a walk in the gardens. Home to several non-profit conservation organizations, including the Santa Monica Mountains Conservancy, the River Center was borne out of a defunct Southern California icon. The Lawry's California Center, once a hip place to dine, had gone bust leaving behind its corporate buildings on a property reminiscent of a Spanish-style estate. After being dormant for seven years, a deal was struck that gave Home Depot part of the property and brought jobs back to the community. The other half, with courtyards, fountains and gardens, became a tribute to the history of the LA River and a botanical haven. Visit the exhibit hall that celebrates the LA River, a natural waterway that still flows over its now concrete bottom. Stroll the gardens with tropical plants, shade trees, colorful annuals, seasonal perennials and blooming roses. Discover the peace a green space offers in the middle of a city.

ADMISSION: FREE
HOURS: Sunrise to Sunset (garden) 8:30AM to 9PM Mon — Fri, 9AM to 5PM Sat & Sun (center)
PARKING: Street * **THOMAS GUIDE:** 594 J6
KID-FRIENDLY * **WHEELCHAIR/STROLLER ACCESS**

Maguire Gardens

LA CENTRAL LIBRARY
Fifth and Flower Sts, Los Angeles 90071
213-228-7000
www.lapl.org/central/tours.html

During World War II, Americans planted victory gardens to help conserve food and build solidarity. Maguire Gardens is a victory garden, too. But unlike those planted in the early 1940s, this garden celebrates triumph over a devastating fire. The urban oasis, perched atop the garage at the LA Central Library is named for developer Robert F. Maguire III, who helped lead the charge to restore the library after the 1986 blaze that destroyed much of the building and its collections. The 1.5-acre garden's themes—literacy and liberty—are reflected in its works of art and design. The Italianate reflecting pool and adjacent steps combine to form "The Spine" of a book. The "Well of Scribes" sculpture forms a tome's title page. And the grotto fountain includes the text of the U.S. Constitution's Fourteenth Amendment. Readers and other seekers of quiet are sheltered from the sights and sounds of nearby traffic by rows of trees standing along the winding pathways.

ADMISSION: FREE
PARKING: Pay structure, fee varies by day and time
THOMAS GUIDE: 634 E4
KID-FRIENDLY * **WHEELCHAIR/STROLLER ACCESS**

Mildred E. Mathias Botanical Garden

UCLA
405 Hilgard Ave, LA 90095
310- 825-1260
www.botgard.ucla.edu

Discover one of the nation's most important botanical collections, an outdoor biology classroom and an open-to-the-public living museum all in one. With 5,000 subtropical plants from 225 different species on 7 acres, the UCLA botanical haven offers visitors a close look at a carefully cultivated and notated garden. Records of the growing specimens are kept and students, professional botanists and horticulturalists study the plants. Because this pocket of land is mostly frost-free, the university is able to propagate plants that cannot be grown outdoors elsewhere in the US. No recreational activities are allowed here and you may come across an outdoor study session, so quiet is required. Located on the campus' southeastern corner, the main entrance is on Tiverton Ave., near the hospital Emergency Center.

ADMISSION: FREE
HOURS: 8AM to 5PM Mon – Fri (winter closing 4PM), 8AM to 4PM Sat - Sun. Closed University holidays.
PARKING: $7 campus lots * **THOMAS GUIDE:** 631 J1

Orcutt Ranch Horticulture Center

23600 Roscoe Blvd, West Hills 91304
818-346-7449
www.laparks.com

Escape urban chaos at Rancho Sombre del Roble (ranch shaded by the oak) also known as Orcutt Ranch. In the 1920s this verdant space became the summer home of Union Oil VP William Orcutt and his wife Mary. Their hacienda-style adobe house is still surrounded by coastal live oaks, including a giant that's 700+ years old. Once a 200-acre estate, the LA city-owned park contains 24 of the original acres with a bamboo grove, exotic shrubs and rose gardens. The 500 rose bushes come with names such as Double Delight, Tropicana and Rio Sombre. Citrus groves provide pickable Valencia oranges and white grapefruits. For one weekend in July, fresh fruit seekers can pick their own, filling a grocery bag for $2 or a medium sized box for $5. You can rent a fruit picker for $1. Take a FREE docent-led tour of the ranch house the last Sunday of the month.

ADMISSION: FREE * **HOURS:** Sunrise to Sunset
PARKING: FREE * **THOMAS GUIDE:** 529 F2
KID-FRIENDLY * HISTORIC * WHEELCHAIR/STROLLER ACCESS

Pageant of Roses Garden

ROSE HILLS MEMORIAL PARK
3888 S Workman Mill Rd, Whittier 90601
562-699-0921
www.rosehills.com

Inhale the sweet scent of thousands of roses at this 1,400-acre cemetery's popular 3.5-acre rose garden. Opened in 1959, the lushly landscaped award-winning garden features 7,000 rose bushes with more than 600 varieties. An official display garden for both the American Rose Society and the All-America Rose Selections, you'll find unusual and stunning examples from the oldest known moss rose to the current All-America title winners. Look for the miniature roses that line many of the rose beds. The memorial park offers a self-guided tour map of its gardens, found at the front gate information booth.

ADMISSION: FREE * **HOURS:** 8AM to dusk, daily
PARKING: FREE * **THOMAS GUIDE:** 677 C1
KID-FRIENDLY * **WHEELCHAIR/STROLLER ACCESSIBLE**

Pine Wind Japanese Garden

TORRANCE CULTURAL ARTS CENTER
3330 Civic Center Dr, Torrance 90503
310-781-7150
www.tcad.torrnet.com

Experience 10,000 square feet of tranquility in *Sho Fu En* an authentically designed Japanese Garden, the "jewel in the crown" of the Torrance Cultural Arts Center. Noted Japanese landscape architect Takeo Uesugi created a balanced design of plants, waterscapes, stones and architecture. Several tree varieties provide shade and beauty including Japanese Flowering Cherry, Saucer Magnolia and Purple Leaf Plum. A koi pond also attracts wild ducks, geese, bullfrogs and turtles. Funded by Epson/Seiko of

Japan and Epson America, Inc., the garden is a reminder of the community's relationship with Japan sister city, Kashiwa.

HOURS: 8AM to dusk Mon. – Sat, 10AM to dusk Sun.
Closed rainy days and during private parties
ADMISSION: FREE
PARKING: FREE * **THOMAS GUIDE:** 765 E5
WHEELCHAIR/STROLLER ACCESS: partial

Rancho Santa Ana Botanic Gardens

1500 N College Ave, Claremont 91711
909-625-8767
www.rsabg.org

Commune with nature in a setting of 6,000 different plants on 86 acres. The natural gardens specialize in growing and developing plants that thrive in California's Mediterranean climate of dry summers and wet winters. Any season is a good time for a visit, but spring puts on a show of riotous color when the wildflowers, perennials and shrubs are in full bloom. The gardens also feature a diverse variety of wildlife and birds. The Audubon Society conducts a bird walk on the first Sunday of each month. Docent-led garden tours are available on weekends at 2PM. Admission is FREE, but a donation is encouraged.

ADMISSION: FREE
HOURS: 8AM to 5PM daily. Closed July 4th; Thanksgiving Day;
Christmas Day and New Year's Day.
PARKING: FREE * **THOMAS GUIDE:** 601 D1
KID FRIENDLY

Self-Realization Fellowship Temple Lake Shrine

17190 Sunset Blvd, Pacific Palisades 90272
310-454-4114
www.yogananda-srf.org/temples/

Modern science has recently discovered what ancient Eastern philosophers have known for centuries: time set aside for introspection and solitude are vital for our mental wellbeing. Whether that quiet time is used in prayer, meditation, or a peaceful stroll, this Shrine provides the perfect environment for accessing our higher selves. Dedicated by Paramahansa Yogananda in 1950, the 10-acre Shrine includes a museum of his work, a natural spring-fed lake, a fern grotto, waterfalls, and lush gardens. Even the fauna, including white swans, ducks, and koi are here to promote feelings of serenity. The Court of Religions features symbols of the world's five great faiths and the Gandhi World Peace Memorial is located under the landmark Golden Lotus Archway. Statues of Krishna, Jesus, and St. Francis of Assisi bear witness to the founders' religious tolerance.

ADMISSION: FREE
PARKING: FREE lot (closed Sunday mornings except to those attending services)
THOMAS GUIDE: 630 G5

Self-Realization Fellowship, The Mother Center

3880 San Raphael Ave, LA 90065
323-225-2471
www.yogananda-srf.org/temples/

Most of the listings in this book guide you to places to see and activities to do. Here is a place to just be. Established in 1925 by Paramahansa Yogananda, The Mother Center

provides several botanical spaces for prayer or quiet con-
templation. Located just five miles from Downtown LA
on the crest of Mt. Washington, the center seems light
years away when you find yourself in one of its lush
gardens or under the outdoor grove known as the "temple
of leaves." The chapel is open daily for prayer or meditation. Visitors are treated to panoramic views of various
sections of LA depending upon your vantage point. Please
note that although the Mother Center is open to the public,
it houses administrative offices only and does not hold
public services.

ADMISSION: FREE
HOURS: 9AM to 5PM, Tue – Sat, 1PM to 5PM Sun, closed Mon
PARKING: FREE limited parking area, some FREE street parking
THOMAS GUIDE: 565 A4

S. Mark Taper Botanical Garden

LOS ANGELES PIERCE COLLEGE
6201 Winnetka Ave, Woodland Hills 91367
818-719-6465
www.piercecollege.com/offices/garden/

Wander through two acres of Mediterranean flora located
smack in the middle of a community college campus.
Formerly the grassy quad, the garden was completed in
2003 and serves as an outdoor botanical lab for Pierce
biology students as well as a model for planting for water
conservation. The garden features sections for coastal
sage and chaparral, 300 species of cacti and other succu-
lents, pond and riparian plants, California Channel Island
natives, bird and butterfly-attracting varieties, and native
California shade plants. A massive stone fountain, a
marsh with three solar-powered fountains and a desert
stream tumbling over rocks, add a soothing supplement of
sounds to the visual beauty of the garden. Planned addi-

tions include Australian and South African natives, an evolution walk, shade structures, and a natural stone amphitheater.

ADMISSION: FREE * **HOURS:** Sunrise to Sunset
PARKING: Obtain a day pass from the campus' sheriff's department or park in metered in lot #1 off Calvert St, 25¢ for 20 minutes. No pass required on weekends and holidays.
THOMAS GUIDE: 530 D7

Theodore Payne Foundation

10459 Tuxford St, Sun Valley 91352
818-768-1802 (Foundation)
818-768-3533 (Wildflower Hotline Mar - May)
www.theodorepayne.org.

Dedicated to the preservation of California's native plants and wildflowers, the foundation is firmly planted in a 22-acre canyon area in the Northeast San Fernando Valley. The non-profit organization grew out of renowned land-scaper/nurseryman Theodore Payne's love of native plants. Payne, who had a hand in developing many of LA's botanical gardens, cultivated native plants and their seeds and is responsible for making 400+ of these plants available to the public. Visit the foundation's non-profit retail nursery offering 300 of these species, plus books and seeds for sale. Walk though the demonstration garden areas; stroll along Flower Hill, a wildflower nature trail; picnic in a natural wildlife habitat. Tap into their FREE wildflower hotline (818-768-3533) from March to May.

ADMISSION: FREE
HOURS: 8:30AM to 4:30PM Tue – Sat, closed Sun – Mon (Oct to June); 8:30AM to 4:30PM Thu – Sat, closed Sun – Wed (July to Sept)
PARKING: FREE * **THOMAS GUIDE:** 503 B7
KID-FRIENDLY

UCLA Hannah Carter Japanese Garden

10619 Bellagio Rd, LA 90077
310-825-4574
www.japanesegarden.ucla.edu

Tucked in the Bel Air Estates is one of Southern California's most authentic Japanese-style gardens. Donated to UCLA in 1965 by UC Regents Chair Edward W. Carter, the 2-acre hillside retreat was inspired by gardens in Kyoto and originally designed by renowned Japanese architect Nagao Sakuai. The terraced acreage is planted with symbolic artifacts and antiquities including stone statues, pagodas and lanterns imported from Japan. The garden includes a traditional teahouse, a koi pond and water falls. Located about one mile from the UCLA campus, reservations are required and FREE self-guided visits are limited to 50 minutes due to limited parking.

ADMISSION: FREE Reservations required
HOURS: 10AM to 3PM Tue, Wed, Fri. Various closure dates.
PARKING: FREE but limited ∗ **THOMAS GUIDE:** 592 A7

Wayfarers Chapel

5755 Palos Verdes Dr South, Rancho Palos Verdes 90275
310-377-7919
www.wayfarerschapel.org

Some find sanctuary in nature, others in a house of worship. Visitors to Wayfarers Chapel will find a magnificent combination of the two. The chapel is built mostly from glass to take advantage of its location perched above the Pacific and surrounded by redwoods, rolling hills, and wide lawns. The church was designed by Lloyd Wright, son of the legendary Frank Lloyd Wright, with the idea of using nature's beauty as a starting point for finding reverence for God. A longtime favorite venue for weddings and baptisms, the sanctuary is the property of the Swedenborgian Church, although all are welcome to visit the grounds and worship in the chapel. The grounds include a reflection pool, azalea garden, hillside stream, and Forrest Floor Garden, which Lloyd Wright designed to resemble the shaded base of a redwood forest.

ADMISSION: FREE
PARKING: FREE lot * **THOMAS GUIDE:** 823 A4

Wrigley Gardens

TOURNAMENT HOUSE
391 S Orange Grove Blvd, Pasadena 91184
626-449-4100
www.tournamentofroses.com

In a town that calls itself the "City of Roses," it's no surprise to find thousands of the namesakes blooming outside of Tournament House, the official headquarters for the Tournament of Roses. Three gardens, including an English style All-America Rose Selections garden display more than 100 varieties on 2,000 rose bushes, including the rose developed especially for the Tournament of Roses Centennial. The 4.5-acre gardens also include 1,500+ varieties of camellias and annuals, enough to create a few show-stopping Rose Parade floats.

HOURS: Sunrise to sunset, daily * **ADMISSION:** FREE
PARKING: FREE * **THOMAS GUIDE:** 565 G5
KID-FRIENDLY

HISTORIC PLACES

Andres Pico Adobe

10940 Sepulveda Blvd, Mission Hills 91345
818-365-7810
www.sfvhs.com/andrespicoadobe.htm

LA's second oldest adobe house is a living museum with a charmed life. The two-story residence has been rescued twice, once from neglect, and once from the wrecking ball. Built in 1834 by Andres Pico, general of the Mexican-California armed forces, the adobe was added onto from 1846 until the early 1870s. Owned by the Pico family and descendents until the late 19th century, the structure and grounds eventually fell into ruin. In 1930 famed archaeologist Dr. Mark Harrington, former Southwest Museum curator, bought and restored the site. In 1965, when its then-owners considered razing the house, the City of LA purchased it. Now home to its caretaker, the San Fernando Valley Historical Society, the adobe displays beads, artifacts, costumes, clothing and Victorian era furnishings. FREE tours every Monday. Research library available by appointment.

ADMISSION: FREE * **HOURS:** 10AM to 3PM Mon and every 3rd Sun
PARKING: FREE lot * **THOMAS GUIDE:** 501 H2
KID-FRIENDLY

El Alisal (Lummis Home)

200 E Ave 43, Highland Park 90031
323-222-0546
www.socalhistory.org

He walked from Cincinnati to LA in 143 days to take a job as city editor with the LA Times. He served as head librarian of the LA Public Library. He founded the Southwest Museum. He hobnobbed with Teddy Roosevelt, John Muir, Will Rogers, and Carl Sandburg. And even after a stroke left him partially paralyzed, he built El Alisal—a two-story home made only from boulders, concrete, railroad ties, and telegraph poles - with his own two hands. He was Charles Fletcher Lummis, a bigger-than-life character and one of the most fascinating figures in LA history. The house, described by one writer as an example of "castle-hacienda" architecture, was completed in 1910 after 14 years of construction. El Alisal, which means "place of the sycamores," is now a museum dedicated to Lummis' life and work and includes Indian and Southwest art, crafts and photographs. All of the original furniture, made by Lummis himself, is on display, too.

ADMISSION: FREE * **HOURS:** Noon to 4PM, Fri - Sun
PARKING: FREE lot * **THOMAS GUIDE:** 595 B5

El Pueblo de Los Angeles Historical Monument

125 Paseo de la Pueblo, Los Angeles 90012
213-628-3562
www.ci.la.ca.us/ELP
www.olvera-street.com

El Pueblo combines a living museum with a daily fiesta in what is both the oldest section of LA and the contemporary corazon (heart) of the city. The monument is home to world-famous Olvera Street, a Mexican-style marketplace, as well as 11 historically significant buildings open to the public. Stop by the visitor's center and catch the FREE 18-minute film, "Pueblo of Promise," a history of LA's founding and development. Join a FREE two-hour guided tour of the 1818 Avila Adobe, the brick 1855 Pelanconi House, the 1887 Eastlake Victorian Sepulveda House, the oldest Catholic Church in LA and the Fire House Museum with its turn-of-the-century fire fighting equipment. Or pick up the FREE self-guided tour brochure. Then step out onto Olvera Street. With mariachis and other musicians serenading you, browse shops and stalls for crafts, clothing, and jewelry. Sample genuine Mexican cuisine at one of four sit-down restaurants or 14 eateries selling snacks and sweets.

ADMISSION: FREE * **HOURS:** 10AM to 7PM, daily
GUIDED TOURS: 10AM, 11AM, Noon, Tue - Sat
PARKING: $5 adjacent lots or at Union Station * **THOMAS GUIDE:** 634 G3
KID-FRIENDLY * **WHEELCHAIR/STROLLER ACCESS**

El Molino Viejo ("The Old Mill")

1120 Old Mill Rd, San Marino 91109
www.oldmill.info

Cruise down San Marino's Old Mill Road, a street lined with oak trees and old-money homes, and, in spite of the name, the last thing you'd expect to find is a gristmill. And yet, smack dab in the middle of a palatial San Marino neighborhood stands the "Old Mill," the oldest commercial structure in Southern California. Built in 1816 by San Gabriel Mission Indians, this California historic landmark housed the area's first water-powered mill. Today, most of the mill is gone, but the adobe building that enclosed it still stands. Mature oak and fruit trees and rustic gardens with meandering paths surround the courtyards. Inside, visit historical exhibits and catch the latest plein air paintings at the California Art Club exhibits in the granary room. The Old Mill is less than five minutes away from the Huntington Library, Art Collections & Botanical Gardens.

ADMISSION: FREE
HOURS: 1PM to 4PM Tue – Sun; closed Mon and holidays
PARKING: FREE on street * **THOMAS GUIDE:** 596 B1
KID FRIENDLY

Heritage Junction Historic Park

24107 San Fernando Rd, Newhall 91321
661-254-1275
www.scvhs.org

Step into yesteryear at this collection of rescued historic buildings, a rose garden and other treasures from the past. See the restored Saugus Train Station, which the Santa Clarita Valley Historical Society acquired from Southern Pacific Railroad in 1980. Now the society's headquarters and a museum that showcases local history, the station dates back to September 1, 1887 when a spur line to Ventura was completed. Mogul Steam Engine 1629 sits alongside the station, a gift from Gene Autry in 1982. It had been at Melody Ranch, an old western movie studio in the area. Visit the Mitchell Schoolhouse Adobe, LA County's second oldest school. Historical society members retrieved adobe bricks from the original structure, which stood at Mitchell Ranch in Sulphur Springs, but was demolished. After picking up all the pieces, historical society members put them back together.

ADMISSION: FREE * **HOURS:** 1PM to 4PM Sat-Sun, except holidays
PARKING: FREE * **THOMAS GUIDE:** 4641 A2
KID FRIENDLY

LA Central Library

630 W Fifth St, LA 90071
213-228-7000
www.lapl.org/central

With FREE admission, FREE book borrowing, and FREE Internet access, libraries are the ultimate FREEbies. Throw in the largest book collection west of the Mississippi and museum-quality art and architecture, and you have LA's Central Library. Opened in 1926, the library has over 6 million books (including a children's collection of 250,000) and 63 computers with Internet and word processing capabilities. FREE daily docent-led tours of the historic library that survived a devastating fire in 1986 and re-opened in 1993 following renovation and expansion. Discover incredible artwork including 12 murals featuring LA's history, a brilliantly-painted 36' by 36' ceiling, three magnificent bronze chandeliers and a marble-and-metal "Statue of Civilization." The Children's Court features the Lotus Shaft Fountain and panel carvings of famous kids' book characters. The library also has a children's theater and a folk doll collection. Pick up the library's FREE event schedule or check the calendar on the Web.

ADMISSION: FREE
HOURS: 10AM to 8PM Mon – Thu, 10AM to 6PM Fri – Sat,
1PM to 5PM Sun
TOURS: Walk-in for 10 people or less, 12:30PM Mon – Fri,
11AM & 2PM Sat, 2PM Sun
PARKING: Special validated rates with LAPL card if presented to library
info desk during library service hours
THOMAS GUIDE: 634 E4
KID-FRIENDLY * **WHEELCHAIR/STROLLER ACCESS**

Los Encinos State Historical Park

16756 Moorpark St., Encino, CA 91436
818-784-4849
www.lahacal.org/losencinos.html

Visit a five-acre microcosm of San Fernando Valley history
in a peaceful setting. Located just steps from bustling
Ventura Blvd, Los Encinos is often overlooked by those driving by. Discover two historical houses, a guitar-shaped
duck pond fed by a natural spring and exhibits of early life
on this ranch. The Tongva Indians lived here for possibly
thousands of years before Spanish missionaries took over
in the early 1800s. The De La Osa Adobe was built in 1849
and the limestone Garnier House was added 20 years later.
Both are currently closed for repairs. The site is an archae-
ological goldmine—nearly one million artifacts have been
found here. Come on the third Sunday of every month to
experience a Living History Day. The Los Encinos Docents
dress in 19th Century clothing, play old-time music,
demonstrate traditional crafts like blacksmithing and offer
children's games and other activities. The park is also a
popular setting for weddings, picnics, and parties.

ADMISSION: FREE
HOURS: 10AM to 5PM Wed – Sun;
Living History Day 1PM to 3PM, 3rd Sun every month
PARKING: FREE on street * **THOMAS GUIDE:** 561 D3

Mentryville & the Felton Schoolhouse

27201 Pico Canyon Rd, Newhall 91381
661-799-1198 (City of Santa Clarita)
www.scvhistory.com/mentryville/index.htm

California boomed more than a century ago when pioneers from across the nation headed west in search of black gold and struck lucrative oil fields. Walk the grounds that once produced gushers at Mentryville, now a ghost town. According to legend, the historic site situated in Santa Clarita Woodlands Park—just a stone's throw from Six Flags Magic Mountain—became California's first oil town. French immigrant Charles Alexander Mentry relocated to the Pico Canyon area from Pennsylvania. Mentry drilled a well, which produced a gusher that shot 65 feet into the air on September 26, 1876. That well averaged 30 barrels of oil daily for many years. Now docents lead visitors through the site, which by 1880 served as home to about 100 families. While single men lived in bunkhouses and families dwelled in clapboard cabins, the Mentry family occupied a 13-room Victorian mansion. In 1885, town residents constructed the little red Felton Schoolhouse, named after future U.S. Senator Charles N. Felton, then-president of Pacific Coast Oil. The town went into decline in the early 1900s and Mentryville eventually turned into a ghost town. Tours are available from Noon to 4PM the first and third Sundays of each month.

ADMISSION: FREE
TOURS: Noon to 4PM, 1st & 3rd Sun each month
PARKING: FREE * **THOMAS GUIDE:** 4640 A1
KID-FRIENDLY * **WHEELCHAIR/STROLLER ACCESS**

Paramount Ranch

Paramount Ranch Rd (off Cornell Rd), Agoura Hills 91301
818-597-9192
www.nps.gov/samo/maps/para.htm

Explore one of the few working movie ranches still in use in Southern California. Since 1927, Paramount Ranch has been used by most of the major Hollywood studios to pose as locations as diverse as Tombstone, Arizona; Dodge City, Kansas; a South Seas island; suburban Boston; the Ozarks; and ancient China. John Wayne, Cary Grant, Kirk Douglas, Lucille Ball, Susan Hayward, and Diane Keaton worked here on motion pictures such as Gunfight at the OK Corral, The Virginian, Gunsmoke, The Adventures of Tom Sawyer, and Reds. Most recently, the ranch was home to the hit series Dr. Quinn, Medicine Woman and still retains the Western Town set used in that series. The ranch has restrooms, picnic tables and several hiking trails.

ADMISSION: FREE * **HOURS:** Sunrise to Sunset
PARKING: FREE * **THOMAS GUIDE:** 588 B3
KID-FRIENDLY * **WHEELCHAIR/STROLLER ACCESS**

Santa Susana Pass State Historic Park

Access at Chatsworth Park South
22360 Devonshire St, Chatsworth 91311
310-455-2465
www.parks.ca.gov

Perched on a series of ridges tucked between the Santa Susana Mountains and the Simi Hills, this 670-acre park is rich in history and wildlife, and boasts spectacular views to boot. The artistically talented Tongva and Chumash Indian tribes lived here and their descendents, who still reside in the area, have continued their tradition of creative expression. Stagecoaches bound for points north began rolling through the pass in 1860 and continued over the next 30 years using a path now known as Stagecoach Road, one of the many hiking trails crisscrossing the park. Hikers reaching the ridge tops are rewarded with vistas of the suburban communities of the San Fernando Valley to the south and east and of the windswept, wild hills of Eastern Simi Valley to the west. Two streams produce seasonal waterfalls and though close to civilization, the park is home to mule deer, bobcats, coyotes, and gray foxes.

ADMISSION: FREE * **HOURS:** 8AM to Sunset
PARKING: FREE lot Chatsworth Park South,
22360 Devonshire St, Chatsworth
THOMAS GUIDE: 499 G/H 2-5
KID-FRIENDLY

Tournament of Roses House

391 South Orange Grove Blvd, Pasadena 91184
626-449-4100
www.tournamentofroses.com

If you love architecture, history and gardens as much as a good parade, head to Tournament House, official headquarters of the Tournament of Roses. Learn about the 115-year history of the Rose Parade while exploring the elaborate, 18,500-square foot Italian Renaissance mansion, once home to chewing gum magnate William Wrigley. The ornate manse features inlaid marble floors, crystal light fixtures and real wood paneling. Don't miss the exhibit of crowns and tiaras worn by former Rose Queens and Princesses. Take a FREE guided tour on Thursdays at 2PM and 3PM. Then take time to stop and smell the roses in Wrigley Gardens, a 4.5-acre floral extravaganza with 1,500 varieties of roses, camellias and annuals—enough to cover at least one Rose Parade float.

HOURS: FREE guided tours 2PM & 3PM Thu, Feb to Aug;
self-guided tours 2PM – 4PM
PARKING: FREE * **THOMAS GUIDE:** 565 G5

Will Rogers State Historical Park

1501 Will Rogers State Park Rd, Pacific Palisades 90272
310-454-8212
www.parks.ca.gov

Humorist Will Rogers said that he never met a man he didn't like, but if you visit this 186-acre Westside Park, you'll see that Rogers obviously had similar feelings for horses. The famed actor, radio personality, author and rodeo performer built his home on this site and lived here from 1924 until his death in 1935. His love of equine activities still permeates the house and grounds. The park contains the only regulation size outdoor polo field in LA County and polo matches are still held here most weekends. The stables behind the main house have been renovated and still house horses. Trails built for humans and horses alike, lead to some of the most breathtaking views in LA. The main ranch house where Rogers and his family lived contains the original furniture and furnishings. The visitor's center, once a guesthouse, presents a short film of Rogers's life. Note that the main ranch house will be closed for renovations until late 2004.

ADMISSION: FREE
HOURS: (Park) 8AM to Sunset daily
(Polo Games) 2PM to 5PM Sat, 10AM to 2PM Sun, May to Sept
PARKING: $6 lot, extremely limited FREE street parking
THOMAS GUIDE: 631 C4
KID-FRIENDLY * **WHEELCHAIR/STROLLER ACCESS**

Ahmanson Ranch Park

N end of Las Virgenes Rd, Calabasas 91302
818-878-4225
www.cityofcalabasas.com

This 2,983-acre park was the object of a 17-year battle between a coalition of community activists, environmentalists and conservationists vs. Washington Mutual and its predecessor, The Ahmanson Corporation, who wanted to build 3,000 homes on the site. In late 2003, WaMu sold the land to the State of California, which assigned management of the park to the Santa Monica Mountains Conservancy for use as a permanent wildlife refuge and natural parkland. Fifteen miles of trails and dirt roads wind through gently rolling hills covered with heritage oaks, coastal sage, and native grasses. Seasonal streams flow near many of the trails. Dogs on leashes are permitted. Several classic movies were filmed here including *Gone With the Wind, The Charge of the Light Brigade,* and *They Died With Their Boots On.*

ADMISSION: FREE * **HOURS:** FREE
PARKING: FREE street on Las Virgenes Rd;
at west end of Victory Blvd in Woodland Hills by the end of 2004.
THOMAS GUIDE: 558 G-J 1&2
KID-FRIENDLY * **HISTORIC**

Audubon Center at Debs Park

ERNEST E. DEBS PARK
4700 N Griffin Ave, LA 90031
323-221-2255
www.audubon-ca.org/debs_park.htm

Enter Northeast LA's gateway to nature and wildlife at the
National Audubon Society's newest urban facility. Only the
second such nature center in the US, it provides city
residents, especially children, with a hands-on outdoor
experience. From bugs to birds to butterflies, the 17-acre
educational site inside the 282-acre hillside park helps
visitors explore the natural habitat that still exists despite
urbanization. Pet Fluffy, a domesticated gopher snake; pot
plants in the 3/4-acre Children's Garden; and hike to find
some of the park's 130+ bird species. Take advantage of
the Backpack Loan Program that offers visitors exploration
essentials including binoculars and trail guides.

ADMISSION: FREE * **HOURS:** 10AM to 6PM daily
PARKING: FREE * **THOMAS GUIDE:** 595 B4
KID-FRIENDLY * **WHEELCHAIR/STROLLER ACCESS**

Eaton Canyon Nature Center

1750 N Altadena Dr, Pasadena 91107
626-398-5420
www.ecnca.org

Explore the San Gabriel foothills at this 190-acre nature
area. Named after Judge Eaton, the man who first used
irrigation to grow grapes on these slopes, the 7,600-

square-foot nature center has live canyon animals on display including a scorpion, tree frog, toad, western fence lizard, alligator lizard, king snake, rosy boa and rattlesnake. Other displays include plants, geology, canyon history and ecology. See plaster casts of animal tracks, billion-year-old rocks and a preserved great horned owl. A perfect starting point for hikes the center offers FREE pamphlets and maps of the area, including hiking trails. Sign-up for the docent-led moonlit walks on Friday nights for only $2 per person.

ADMISSION: FREE ★ **HOURS:** 9AM to 5PM daily
PARKING: FREE ★ **THOMAS GUIDE:** 536 E7
KID-FRIENDLY ★ **WHEELCHAIR/STROLLER ACCESS**

El Dorado Nature Center

EL DORADO PARK EAST
7550 E Spring St, Long Beach 90815
562-570-1745
www.ci.long-beach.ca.us

Nestled in the eastern half of El Dorado Park is "an island of serenity in the midst of the busy urban landscape." The 102.5-acre nature center is a wildlife oasis with wetlands, meadows and forests. Explore the two miles of dirt trail or the quarter mile of paved trail (both wheelchair and stroller accessible), dip your toes in a stream or go fishing in the two lakes. Keep your eyes out for wild animals including hawks, turtles, foxes and weasels. Visit the interactive exhibits at the museum, which include some live animal display. Sign up for a nature center program. Most are low cost ($5 or less per person); some are free such as Simple Saturdays, an environmental awareness day the 2nd Saturday of each month; monthly art exhibits; reptile shows and summer concerts.

ADMISSION: FREE
HOURS: (Trails) 8AM to 5PM Tue – Sun
(Museum) 10AM to 4PM Tue – Fri, 8:30AM to 4PM Sat - Sun

PARKING: $3 per vehicle, weekdays; $5 per vehicle, weekends
THOMAS GUIDE: 796 G2
KID-FRIENDLY * WHEELCHAIR/STROLLER ACCESS

John Panatier Nature Center

WILDERNESS PARK

2240 Highland Oaks Dr, Arcadia 91006
626-355-5309
www.ci.arcadia.ca.us

Discover wildlife at the foot of the San Gabriel Mountains at this 120-acre park located below Big Santa Anita Canyon. Most of the park is still in its natural state, with about 9 acres set aside for recreational use, including the nature center. Check out the live reptiles on display, look at preserved wildlife exhibits and observe mosquito fish in the center's new water feature. Open weekdays, the park and nature center are open by reservation only on the weekends. Groups can schedule FREE nature talks weekdays only.

ADMISSION: FREE except for groups of 11+
HOURS: 8:30AM to 4:30PM Mon – Fri (Oct to Apr),
8:30AM to 7PM Mon - Fri (May-Sept)
PARKING: FREE * **THOMAS GUIDE:** 537 E7
KID-FRIENDLY

Madrona Marsh Nature Center and Preserve

3201 Plaza del Amo, Torrance 90503
310-782-3989
www.friendsofmadronamarsh.com

Explore the only vernal marsh left in LA County—a natural depression which floods during the rainy season and a habitat that hosts a wealth of wildlife. Among the visitors to the 10-acre lowland marsh area and its upper back dune system with vernal pools: ducks, coots, hawks, red-winged blackbirds, Pacific tree frogs, butterflies and dragonflies. The preserve is open year-round but wildlife is most abundant during the winter and spring; the wetland dries out in summer. Across the street, the 8,000-square-foot nature center offers educational programs and features exhibits, a native garden and a gift shop. The Friends of Madrona Marsh sponsors monthly habitat restoration days.

ADMISSION: FREE * **HOURS:** 10AM to 5PM daily; closed some holidays
PARKING: FREE * **THOMAS GUIDE:** 763 E7
KID-FRIENDLY

Placerita Canyon Park & Nature Center

19152 Placerita Canyon Road, Newhall 91321
661-259-7721
www.placerita.org

Take a hike to the site of California's original gold discovery—The Oak of the Golden Dream—where Francisco Lopez y Arballo found golden flakes clinging to wild onions roots in 1842. The 350-acre natural park's 10 miles of hiking trails include paved routes for parents pushing strollers and wheelchair visitors. Year-round activities offer something for the entire family, set against a backdrop of beautiful oak groves and a seasonal stream lined with willow and sycamore trees. A waterfall flows from January until May. Visit Walker's Cabin, an early frontier home; look at wildlife displays and pack a lunch for the picnic area.

ADMISSION: FREE * **HOURS:** 9AM to 5PM daily
PARKING: FREE * **THOMAS GUIDE:** 4641 G1
KID-FRIENDLY

Vasquez Rocks County Park

10700 W Escondido Canyon Rd, Agua Dulce 91350
661-268-0840
http://parks.co.la.ca.us

Marvel at the high desert's unique geological formations—
2,500-feet high—near Agua Dulce Springs. Nestled in 745
acres around Soledad basin, these breathtaking rock formations are a result of the earthquake rattling the region
for millions of years. The dramatic beauty that attracts
numerous artists has been used in various film and television productions, including *Star Trek*, *Bonanza* and the
original Austin Powers movie. In fact, screen legend
Rudolph Valentino is said to have starred in the first movie
ever filmed here in the early 1900s. Get a first-hand look at
the geology and plant and animal life during FREE ranger-
led hikes every Sunday at 11AM. Walk through time on the
park's history trail and learn about the Tataviam Native
American tribe and Spanish settlers who dwelled here.
Although the area draws rock climbers, skilled hikers and
horseback riders, it's not recommend for young children.

ADMISSION: FREE
HOURS: Daylight hours; some overnight camping allowed
PARKING: FREE * **THOMAS GUIDE:** 4373 E7
NOT RECOMMENDED FOR YOUNG CHILDREN

Whittier Narrows Nature Center

1000 N Durfee Ave, South El Monte 91733
626-575-5523
http://parks.co.la.ca.us

Discover the vast array of bird nests at the nature center
tucked inside a 200-acre natural woodland. A former film
location for such films as *Tarzan and His Mate* (1934, starring Johnny Weissmuller), this wildlife area is a popular
birding spot. Featuring four lakes, the area is a winter

sanctuary for migrating waterfowl. Visit the exhibits at the nature center, which highlight the woodland's river environment including live plant and animal life. Operated by the LA County Department of Parks & Recreation, the nature center offers low cost ranger tours, bird walks and other programs. Take a hayride Saturday mornings for only $1 per child and $2 per adult.

ADMISSION: FREE * **HOURS:** 9:30AM to 5PM daily
PARKING: FREE * **THOMAS GUIDE:** 637 C6
KID-FRIENDLY * **WHEELCHAIR/STROLLER ACCESS**

Indexes

MAIN INDEX

LOCATION INDEX

There are several communities within the boundaries of the City of LA, and several more surrounding the city. All are included in *FREE L.A.* Use this Location Index to find FREE fun by community or location. Each community includes the Thomas Guide Page(s) for that area and the pages in *FREE L.A.* that feature an event or venue in that location.

About the Contributors

ROBERT STOCK is a Los Angeles native. He has done news, sports, business, and public relations writing for over 10 years and teaches business writing at Pierce College. An avid basketball fan and player, he enjoys hiking, cooking, and reading. He also likes to tend his garden using the FREE compost from the Las Virgenes Water District. He lives in Calabasas with his wife Linda and daughter Sara.

ALISHA L. SEMCHUCK, a Chicago native, now resides in Southern California where she works as a staff writer for Palmdale's *Antelope Valley Press*. She entered journalism in the mid '80s, initially reporting for a weekly paper in Lake Zurich, Illinois before joining the staff of several California papers including the *Ventura County Star*. She loves warm and fuzzy animal stories.

A native of Los Angeles, **JOE TORTOMASI** has written for *Westways Magazine*, the *Orange County Register* and the *Los Angeles Times*. For a look at his humorous essays on the Web, explore http://homepage@mac.com/torto/.

Recently he has been following the Seabiscuit saga. Until his literary ship comes in, the author can be reached through his bookie.

SUSAN CARRIER migrated from West Virginia to Southern California immediately after college 28 years ago. She loves exploring the area's diverse neighborhoods and cultural attractions and frequently writes about them for *Sunset Magazine* and the *Los Angeles Times,* as well as other publications. She lives in Altadena with her husband, teenage daughter, a dog and a cat.

A produced playwright and published short story writer, **DESIREE ZAMORANO** teaches Multicultural Ed to teachers, and writing to elementary students in between writing novels. She loves her native Southern California and is always up for a FREE event with her husband and children.

Though born in Montreal, Quebec, **RON O'BRIEN** is virtually a native Californian. He knows the Golden State intimately, having lived and worked in Northern, Central and Southern California for more than four decades. A Grammy-nominated producer & music historian, he has written extensively for major record labels and produced numerous historical albums. An LA Kings fan, he still plays ice hockey weekly in a local adult league. He lives with his partner Troy and their two children, Tristan & Emelia, in Ojai.

About the Editor

An LA resident for more than 25 years, **TROY CORLEY** has written about the area for numerous publications including *FamilyFun, Parents, Travel & Leisure Family* and *LA Parent* magazines as well as the *Los Angeles Times.* She has taken her family on numerous *FREE L.A.* adventures and has published the travel guide as a way to share them. *FREE L.A.* is the first in a series of FREE Fun Guides.™ Her independent publishing company has other books in the works, as well.

About CorleyGuide™ & Corley Publications

CORLEYGUIDE is a new travel book brand for readers who want "Travel With a Twist." *FREE L.A. The Ultimate Free Fun Guide™ to the City of Angels,* is the first title released under the CorleyGuide name and the first in a series of FREE Fun Guides.™ For more information about the company or *FREE L.A.* visit www.freela.net or www.corleyguide.com.

Independent publishing company, **CORLEY PUBLICATIONS**, was launched in 2002 with the successful release of the unique travel guide, *Let's Go Buggy! The Ultimate Family Guide to Insect Zoos & Butterfly Houses.* For more information or to order copies of *Let's Go Buggy!* visit www.letsgobuggy.com.

Visit us on the Web or contact us at:

CORLEY PUBLICATIONS
P.O. Box 381
Ojai, CA 93024
805-646-5467
FAX: 877-376-2668
Email: Publisher@corleyguide.com

Give friends the gift of FREE fun.
Order them a copy of FREE L.A.!

Yes, I want _____ copies of *FREE L.A. The Ultimate Free Fun Guide to the City of Angels.*

Each copy is $12.95. Add $4 for US Priority Mail for one book (plus $1 for each additional book). California residents add 94 cents sales tax per book.

My check or money order for _____ is enclosed.

My Credit Card Number: _____

Expiration Date: _____

Signature: _____

Name: _____

Organization: _____

Address: _____

City/State/Zip: _____

Billing address for credit card if different from above:

_____

Phone: _____

Email: _____

Please make your check or money order
or credit card payable to:

CORLEY PUBLICATIONS
P.O. Box 381
Ojai, CA 93024
805-646-5467
FAX: 877-376-2668
Email: Booksales@freela.net
www.freela.net

Know of a FREE
fun event or place to go
that's not listed
in FREE L.A.?

*

Please contact us so we can
include it in a future edition.

*

Visit us on the Web at
www.freela.net
and click on the
section asking for new
FREE fun things to do.

*

Or Email us at
info@freela.net

*

You can write or call us, too:
FREE L.A.
P.O. Box 381
Ojai, CA 93024
805-646-5467
FAX: 1-877-376-2668

*